MONSTERS
OF THE
MIDWEST

ACKNOWLEDGEMENTS

The authors would like to thank several people who made this book possible:

The reference librarians and staff, who took us seriously when we asked for assistance with obscure articles and books, especially those at the University of St. Thomas: St. Paul Campus and the Ramsey County Merriam Park Library. While they probably don't get too many patrons looking for primary source support regarding monster legends, we were thankful that they were there to offer some assistance.

The staff of the anthropology department at South Dakota State University, who took the time to answer questions about an obscure blog post and supposed archeological dig. They helped to determine that facts were unsubstantiated, and while we were bummed not to use that story, we were grateful for the help in keeping these stories as authentic as possible.

To Kerry Peterson, for sharing his never-before-published bigfoot sighting. We are thrilled to be able to include something that no one has ever read before.

To Phyllis Galde and to everyone at *FATE Magazine*. Your work and friendship have served as an inspiration on many different levels and helps to make it easier for witnesses of such encounters to feel more comfortable coming forward.

AN IMPORTANT NOTE

Curiosity sometimes leads people to go out looking for ghosts and monsters, but please respect the law, as well as the rights and privacy of others.

Most importantly, we ask anyone who investigates the paranormal to exhibit extreme caution. Do not take this lightly. Tragically, people have died while pursuing legends that we otherwise would have included in this collection. However, a decision was made not to write about those stories here.

Your life is precious, and it is not worth risking. If there is any danger, please, let the legends remain as legends.

Furthermore, the information provided in this book is for reading entertainment purposes only. The author and publisher do not assume and hereby disclaim any liability to any party for any loss, damage or disruption caused by any other use of this information.

TABLE OF CONTENTS

MONSTER CREATURES OF THE WATER

MONSTER CREATURES OF THE AIR

PREFACE

Cryptozoology is the study of legendary animals, or cryptids, that are rumored to live among us but have not yet been proven to exist.

It is human nature to be curious about the unknown. This same curiosity has enabled several beasts, formerly classified as cryptids, to secure a legitimate classification in the animal kingdom. The Komodo dragon, the okapi and even the mountain gorilla are just a few such creatures that were once considered cryptids. At one point, even Florida's beloved manatees were thought by sailors to be real mermaids.

If you are on the skeptical side, remember this when you read these stories: Maybe there really is something else out there, waiting to be discovered and to find its rightful place in the animal kingdom. And maybe . . . it's waiting to strike.

In researching this book, we were struck by something unexpected: the courage of those who lived through the stories. This is not only the bravery required to face these monsters; it's also the courage to come forward to tell of their experiences. We realized, time and again, that these stories come from respected, hard-working members of the community. You will read accounts from doctors and lawyers and from former skeptics and critics. All of these people put their reputations on the line when they decided to talk about their encounters. They faced criticism and ridicule, but still, they spoke up.

And we believe them.

With that said, from newspaper articles, interviews, books and blogs, we've recreated the sightings of some of the most ferocious monster reports of the Midwest. Our research for this book was extensive and thorough. Taking the facts into consideration, we also applied our imagination to each story, often envisioning a scene as it *might* have played out. We strove to provide the details as closely as we were able, giving you, the reader, a glimpse of what it could have been like to be there, in the shoes of a witness. However, in some cases, names have been changed to protect the privacy of individuals.

So curl up for a good read. But maybe you should make sure that your windows and doors are locked first.

—Jessica Freeburg and Natalie Fowler

MONSTER CREATURES
OF THE LAND

THE WENDIGO

Ross Township, Minnesota, Late 1800s

Jake Nelson rounded the corner of the dirt road that led to the Mickinock homestead. His thoughts had been with the family ever since he'd heard that they returned quickly from a hunting trip in Canada, just north of Indian Village, because Mrs. Mickinock was unwell. They were a young family with small children, and Jake wanted to see if there was anything he could do for them. He carried a small basket of food that his wife had prepared.

Mr. Mickinock emerged from the barn, carrying a pail.

"Howdy," said Jake.

Mickinock looked up, a weary expression clouding his face. "Hey, there, Jake," he replied.

"I heard about your missus," Jake said, nodding toward the house solemnly. "I wanted to see how you're doing."

Mickinock set the pail on the ground. Fresh milk sloshed from side to side, nearly spilling over the lip.

"Well, we've been better," he said. "She's been in bed since we got home. She told me before we came back that death had taken control of her." He glanced toward the house then back to Jake. "That's how she said it, Jake, and I believe she might be right. Her skin's so pale you can almost see through it. And she just sleeps all day. The children won't leave her side." He shook his head sadly.

"Well, she has been in our prayers. Your whole family has been," Jake replied. "And we'll keep on praying."

"I appreciate that very much," Mickinock said.

"This is for you and the kids," Jake said, lifting up the basket. "Just some cornbread, jam, an apple pie, stuff my wife thought you all might enjoy."

"Thank you. The kids are missing their mama's good food. I sure can't make much." Mickinock replied. He took the basket in one hand then lifted the pail of milk with the other. "I'd invite you in, but she's sleeping."

Jake nodded and said, "You just holler if you need anything. We're not far down the road."

Mr. Mickinock nodded and smiled sadly, before walking to the house.

As the door closed behind him, Jake looked around the yard. Several pieces of wood were scattered near a chopping stump, and an ax was propped against a nearby tree. He thought for a minute about chopping some more for the family but worried that the sound would wake Mrs. Mickinock. He noticed a small stack of freshly chopped wood neatly piled near the door, and he figured they'd be set for at least a day or two. He decided to stop back tomorrow and see about chopping the rest.

Looking away from the home, something caught his eye in the muddy muskeg just beyond the woodpile. Something seemed to be rising out of the bog.

At first, there were just two bright lights. Much like the orbs he had seen floating around the muskeg behind his own home, they seemed to rise from the marshy ground and float around the trees before fading away. When he'd seen them before, at his own property, his friend Billy

McGillis explained that the lights were from gas, rising out of the marsh.

These orbs were different. They were not floating independently through the air. They were set together in a gaunt face. The face was covered in ashen skin that seemed to be stretched across nothing but jaw and orbital bone. As it rose higher, Jake saw that it was an entire creature. The monster, tall and thin, stood roughly 15 feet high as it emerged from the watery ground. Jake squinted. It appeared to be dressed in . . . white lace.

"A wendigo," he whispered.

He scrambled back and tripped over a stray log. He didn't stop to see if the thing was coming any farther out of the water. He pushed himself back up and ran down the road.

Jake remembered hearing the natives talk about the wendigo creature many times. They claimed it came like a banshee to foretell death. They said a horrible curse fell upon any man who saw it, and that man would resort to eating human flesh for survival. The natives in Indian Village even spoke about a shaman, known as Jack Fiddler, who was said to hunt the wendigos. He lived up in far-northern Ontario.

Could such a creature really exist? By the time he was 100 yards away, Jake began to doubt if he'd seen anything at all. He turned to look back.

To his horror, he still saw the creature, now retreating into the bog. Fear pulsed through his body as he watched it, unable to break his gaze. He felt an urgent, pressing need to know where the monster was going. The thing stumbled, nearly falling as it sloshed through the standing water and rotting vegetation.

Terrified by what he'd seen, Jake turned and ran down the road toward his home.

Would it come after him? Could it really affect him as it had reportedly done to others? Jake didn't stop running until he was safely in his home.

The next morning, he was still shaken by what he had seen, but he had to return. He was determined to help his neighbors any way he could. When he arrived, the children were standing in the front yard, their faces streaked with tears. The doctor stood near the front door, speaking to Mr. Mickinock. Doc patted the poor man's back sympathetically before walking toward the road.

As Doc neared Jake, he shook his head and said, "She passed away this morning."

Jake looked from the doctor to the children, who had just lost their mother, then out at the muskeg behind the small house. He half expected to see the creature looming among the trees, but there was nothing except a gentle breeze rattling the green shrubs that sprouted along the muddy bog.

The wendigo was gone. But with it went a young wife and mother.

Jake wondered again with a shiver if the monster had seen him—and if Jake himself would also be cursed.

* * *

Jack Fiddler, the shaman whom the American Indians of Indian Village had spoken about, was arrested alongside his brother Joseph by Canadian authorities in 1907, for the murder of Joseph's mentally ill daughter-in-law. The men admitted to the crime but claimed she had become a wendigo and, in accordance with tradition, needed to be eliminated to protect others. After being arrested, Jack admitted to killing 14 other people whom he believed had become wendigos.

Before the brothers could be tried and convicted, Jack escaped from prison. He committed suicide by hanging himself from a tree. His brother Joseph was tried and convicted. He died in prison in 1909.

BENTON COUNTY MONSTER SNAKE

Logansport, Indiana, September 1889

There wasn't much remarkable about that afternoon. The wind blew gently, rustling the tree leaves that shaded the gentleman from the sun as he made his way toward home. He passed the cemetery west of Oxford, and something drew his attention to the rows of headstones that marked the final resting spots of Oxford's former citizens.

He wasn't sure if it was the sound that made him look or if he caught a glimpse of movement. But there it was: a 15-foot-long, scale-covered serpent slithering in between the headstones, its belly pressing a path through the grass.

For whatever reason, the man turned to face the snake that slowly but steadily moved toward him. The hair on the back of the man's neck prickled, and his heart nearly stopped as surely as his feet had.

"Lord Almighty," the man gasped. His voice quivered with terror.

The creature was only a few yards away, and it seemed to be picking up speed. Desperately, the man looked around, fearing that the snake would reach him. Within arm's reach, he saw a large stick. Keeping one eye on the slithering monster, he grabbed the stick and held it in front of him.

The serpent began to move toward him even faster.

Looking from the stick to the snake, he feared his stick would be no match for the monstrous serpent. He instead turned and ran toward his house. His legs had never moved so quickly.

He burst through the front door of his home, slamming it shut behind him, his back pressed against it as he wheezed in jagged breaths.

"What on earth . . ." His wife stared at him, eyes wide.

"Nothing," he replied, trying to steady his breath.

The woman raised her brows in suspicion. "Nothing? Look at yourself. You can hardly catch a breath."

"I was just . . ." The man moved to the window and looked out, unable to think of a good reason why he had entered the house in such a panic.

"Was someone after you?" she asked worriedly.

The man said nothing, but he stared out the window, his body still shaking with fear.

"You can't come into this house like you're running for your life and tell me there's nothing going on. Tell me what's got you so shaken."

"In the graveyard . . ." he began, "the snake . . ." He spread his arms as far apart as they would go before putting his hands on his knees. He again tried to steady his breath.

"You saw the ghoul snake?" his wife asked in a whisper, her jaw dropping in a mix of awe and horror.

"It was as wide around as a stovepipe and longer than any two men placed head-to-toe!" He shuddered. "It was coming at me, staring at me with eyes that looked like the flames of a fire. And it had two horns, one on each side of its head, at least 10 inches long!"

"It was coming after you?" His wife hurried to his side and glanced out the window. "Did it follow you home?"

"No . . . I mean, I'm not sure, but I don't think so. I was running too hard to look back."

"You need to tell the sheriff."

* * *

After gathering a group of townsmen, the sheriff, along with the man who reported the sighting, headed toward the cemetery.

"You're not the first to report this thing," the sheriff assured the man. "I've had at least a dozen others come to me in the last two years. Always the graveyard."

"Makes you wonder how a snake around these parts could get so large," one of the men in the group noted.

As they walked through the cemetery gates, the men scanned the area for the creature.

"Look at that hole there," one man said.

"There's another over here," a second called out.

They found a series of large holes leading into the ground around the tombstones.

"I think we've solved the mystery of how a snake could grow so large," one of the men said with a shudder. "That blasted beast is feeding on the poor souls buried here."

THE VAMPIRE OF NEBRASKA

Dawes County, Nebraska, Mid-December 1895

Jack Lewis tipped the collar of his coat up and pulled his hat down against the wind, which rolled across the prairie and seemed to catch at the edge of the gully. He turned in his saddle and glanced back at the roaring campfire. Cookie hung a pot over the fire, and Jack's belly growled at the sight. The others were setting up camp for the night. He'd be back in a minute; he just needed to be alone for a bit first.

"Don't go wandering too far, you hear?" shouted his boss. "Remember that cow we found."

"Yes, sir," Jack answered.

How could he forget? It was a scene like no other. Just this morning, they'd come across a heifer. Her throat was torn open, and blood had spewed all over the fresh snow. For the rest of his life, he would remember the contrast of the bright red blood against the white snow. His hand instinctively felt for his Colt .45.

The worst part about the morning was listening to Charles talk about the mutilated animal for the rest of the ride. This was the first time he'd ever ridden with Charles, and he hoped it would be the last. The man talked about everything, all the time. But today, he talked about blood and mangled cows and how he'd seen a monster-madman attack one of them. He'd told about how the man would knock the creature to the ground then bite and claw at its throat, using incredible strength. After that, the madman would drink his poor victim's blood.

Jack shivered all the way to his toes, and it wasn't because of the December prairie wind. He eased himself out of his saddle and down to the ground. He'd be wise to get back to the others quickly, but he needed a few quiet moments away from Charles's endless chatter. Besides, it wasn't dark yet, and he had his gun. He'd just take a minute or two alone then head back to camp.

Jack kicked at the ground and saw a footprint in the snow. In the light of the setting sun, he bent to take a closer look.

From behind, he heard a branch crack. He spun around and found himself face-to-face with a man whose eyes were wilder than a rabid 'coon's. The man seemed to be foaming from his mouth, which was upturned in a slight, menacing smile.

Before Jack could process what was happening, the strange man lunged and began to claw at Jack's neck. Jack instinctively tried to push the man off, but the man attacked with such ferocity that Jack was no match.

As the beastly attacker alternated between choking and clawing wildly at his throat, Jack drew his gun from his holster. Unable to take aim, he fired off two rounds into the ground, hoping to draw the attention of the other men at camp.

Jack could hear the sounds of feet pounding against the snow and twigs snapping under boots. His comrades rushed to a sight that, most certainly, shocked them. By the time they arrived, the vampire had begun to use his teeth on Jack's throat as if trying to suck his blood.

Jack thrashed wildly beneath the creature, but despite its slim frame, the beast seemed to wield an otherworldly strength that left Jack defenseless.

Hearing the shouts of the others, the vampire leapt from his victim and dashed behind the trees.

"Jack!" His boss stood above him and quickly pressed a handkerchief against his wounded neck.

The others approached, but Jack's boss shouted, "Get after that thing!"

They scrambled to do as they were ordered.

The boss pulled the handkerchief away from Jack's neck. "He got ya good, but they're not too deep. You're going to be fine."

After getting Jack back to the fire, his boss used some boiled water to clean Jack's wounds. Cookie wrapped the gnarled neck in clean dressings that he kept in his knapsack, along with a skin of whiskey. He called that knapsack his "doctoring kit."

As the shock began to wear off, Jack felt an aching that burned in the wounds around his throat and face. He took a long swig from the skin of whiskey.

The sound of hooves coming closer made Jack jump.

Cookie put his hand gently on Jack's shoulder, "It's just our guys coming back."

"I pray they got that sick bastard," the boss said, rising up to meet the men at the edge of camp. "Well?" he shouted as the first of the men drew near.

"Nothing, sir," the man replied. "Once the sun went down, it got too dark to track him. The man—or whatever he was—is gone."

THE MELONHEADS

Kirtland, Ohio, Mid-1970

It was well after midnight when Richard and his buddy Bobby decided to take their girlfriends out to Wisner Road. Rumors of the Melonhead children had enticed them out this way before—but had left them with nothing more than a few goosebumps caused by open windows on a chilly night. They didn't expect to see anything, but it was something to do, and the girls seemed excited to check out a creepy local legend.

As the sound of tires rolling over pavement switched to the grumbling crunch of gravel, Richard found an open spot on the side of the road and pulled off.

"They say Dr. Crowe kept orphaned kids out here and performed awful experiments on them," he said.

"I heard they were children with giant heads," said Bobby's girlfriend, Gail.

"Were they born with giant heads?" Jeanie, Richard's girlfriend, asked. "Or did Dr. Crowe make them that way?"

Richard replied, "I don't know, but whether they came with giant heads or not, they sure had them when he was done with them."

"I heard the kids eventually went crazy and killed Dr. Crowe," Bobby added.

"Can't blame them for that," Gail replied.

Bobby rolled down his window and gazed across the wooded area. The trees had lost their leaves to the autumn weather, and a full moon lit up the open pockets between the thin, reaching branches of the trees.

"Who even knows if all that's true," Jeanie said as she leaned against Richard's shoulder.

"Well, lots of people have seen these things over the years," Bobby said. "How could there be so many sightings if they aren't out here?"

"My older brother knew some guys who saw one watching them from the side of the road. They followed it into the woods," Gail said. "The thing led them to a house where a couple was sitting on the porch, and the man told them he had been a nuclear scientist during World War II. As a result of his work, his children were born with deformed, bulbous heads. The government paid them off to live quietly away from people, but they could never tell anyone about the children."

"Well, if you ask me, it's just an urban legend," Jeanie said, rolling her eyes.

The four sat quietly for a moment, watching the trees around them. A light wind tossed fallen leaves across the ground, causing them to crunch lightly as they hit tree trunks and underbrush. The girls snuggled against the boys to warm up as a cool breeze blew through the open window.

A creepy story plus chilly air—the boys had been down this road, literally, a time or two before with other girls, and the combination seemed to work every time.

"What's that?" Bobby asked, his voice barely above a whisper. He pointed into the trees.

The others followed his gesture.

"Oh, my gosh," Jeanie gasped. "It's one of them. It's a Melonhead."

Gail leaned forward and peered at the creature. It stood about four feet tall beside a tree. Its limbs were unclothed and thin, almost skeletal. Its oversized, hairless head glowed in the moonlight, making it seem even larger and more awkward.

It walked toward a small creek and bent down. Scooping water into its cupped hands, it took a long drink.

Jeanie grabbed Robert's arm. "Get us out of here. What if it sees us?"

The creature turned its large head and looked at them.

"Oh, my gosh, it knows we're here!" she shrieked.

Gail joined Jeanie's panicked pleas. "What if it attacks?"

Bobby reached over and, with trembling hands, rolled up the window.

Robert was so stunned by what he was looking at that he hardly heard the girls' desperate cries. It wasn't until he felt Jeanie shake his arm that he could comprehend what they were saying.

He shifted into drive and whipped the car back in the direction they'd come from. The girls' voices bordered on hysteria as they begged him to hurry.

"Holy cow, man!" Bobby yelled. "We saw one! We actually saw one!"

Robert shook his head in disbelief as they got farther away from the frightening, small being. He didn't want to believe it because it was too creepy, but he couldn't deny what he'd seen.

THE ENFIELD HORROR

Enfield, Illinois, April 25, 1973

The night was clear and unseasonably warm for April in Illinois. Mrs. Garret smiled as her young son, Greg, ran by outside, probably on another imaginary adventure.

"Shouldn't he be in bed by now?" Mr. Garret asked, hardly taking his eyes from the television.

"I'll call him in during the next commercial. It's such a nice night."

Mr. Garret shrugged and returned his full attention to the program. Only a few minutes passed before the screen door swung open and slammed shut with a bang that pulled Mr. Garret's attention from the television.

"Greg," said Mr. Garret, his voice tight with irritation. "You can't come in here slamming doors." He turned to look at his son, intending to scold him, but the look on Greg's face turned his irritation to concern. "What's the matter?" he asked, his tone softening a bit.

"It . . . it . . . it . . ." Greg stammered.

"Are you okay?" Mrs. Garret asked, rushing to her son.

"There's a thing. It had claws . . . and huge eyes. It grabbed at me." Greg's teeth began to chatter.

Mr. Garret strode quickly to the door and peered into the darkness. "I don't see anything."

"It ran that way," said Greg, pointing. He buried his head in his hands.

"Let's get you up to bed," said his mother. She glanced at her husband with a shrug. It wasn't like Greg to make up stories. She ruffled her son's hair and bent down to help him with his shoes. "What happened to your sneakers?" she shrieked. They were torn, shredded across the top.

"It stepped on my feet!" wailed Greg.

"Look," said Mrs. Garret to her husband, her voice a panicked whisper. She held up one of Greg's shoes.

Mr. Garret took what was left of the sneaker. "I'm calling the police."

In the background, their movie broke to commercial. A voice sang a catchy jingle.

* * *

Lil McDaniel sang along with the fun commercial song.

"When do Mom and Dad get home?" asked her brother, Henry, coming in from the kitchen.

"Not sure," said Lil. She flipped off the television, shocking the room into silence. "Probably any minute, which means we should get ready for bed."

"I can't believe we wasted the whole night watching that stupid show. I should have gone to Greg's house."

"You know you can't leave the house when Mom and Dad are gone. Quit complaining. Just hurry up and get to bed before Mom and Dad get home."

"Why are you bossing me around? I'm almost a teenager," Henry said.

"You're only a year older than me," Lil replied.

A bang from the bedroom startled them both.

"What was that?" asked Lil.

"I don't know," said Henry. He went down the hall and peered into the dark room.

"Turn on the light," said Lil behind him.

He felt along the wall until his hand found the switch. The light revealed the mess that their mother had made earlier that evening, trying to find the right outfit to wear to the PTA meeting. But there was nothing in the room that could account for the noise they'd heard.

A soft scratching sound came from the window.

"Do you hear that?" asked Lil.

"Yeah," answered Henry. "It sounds like something is scratching on the AC. It's probably just a cat or a squirrel," he reasoned as he neared the window that held the air conditioning unit.

"Can you see anything?" asked Lil.

"Turn out the light," he instructed. He lifted the corner of the curtain to peek outside.

Lil hurried to her brother's side and stood on her tiptoes. With their heads so close to the AC unit, the scratching sound rattled in their ears.

The scratching stopped. A creature's face appeared on the other side of the glass, peering back at them.

"That's not a cat," Lil shrieked. She ran from the window. "It's got big, pink eyes!"

"It's trying to get in," Henry shouted. "Quick, the other windows, close them!"

Lil raced to her bedroom and slammed her window with a bang that seemed to shake the walls around her. "Lock the front door!" she shouted.

Henry ran down the hall. Lil rushed to Henry's room. Tripping on a baseball bat in the middle of the room, she clamored toward the window, reaching it at the same time as the creature.

Shrieking, she slammed the window shut as the monster's talon-like claws reached up. The beast sliced through the screen and tapped at the glass.

Lil stared, her eyes fixed on the monster. Its hiss was loud enough to hear through the closed window.

"Call Mom and Dad," she yelled as she ran to the kitchen.

Henry was already at the phone, looking for the number that his mother had scribbled into a notebook. The handset trembled in his hand as he twisted the first number into the rotary. The seconds it took to spin the numbers seemed to take minutes.

As he pointed a shaking finger clumsily into the next number, the knob on the front door began to shake. That was followed by a loud pounding.

Lil and Henry looked at each other in horror.

"It's trying to get in!" Lil screamed hysterically.

"Open this door," shouted their father.

"It's Mom and Dad," said Henry, dropping the handset as he ran to the door. "We have to let them in, quick, before it gets them!"

Tears blurred Lil's eyes as her fingers fumbled with the lock. Henry shoved her out of the way and did it himself.

The door flew open, and their father stormed in with their mother behind. Both had scowls on their faces.

"Hurry," said Lil. "Get in here, fast."

She pulled her mother by the hand, and Henry shut the door and locked it again.

"Why was the door locked?" Mr. McDaniel demanded.

"What's wrong, Lilian?" Mrs. McDaniel asked at the very same time.

"There's something out there. Something that's trying to get in," said Lil.

Mrs. McDaniel turned her scowl toward her husband. "I told you not to let them watch that movie last week."

"But this is real," said Henry. "We both saw it. Something is out there, trying to get into the house."

"You're lucky you got in alive. It has sharp claws, and it hissed at me," Lil whispered with a shiver.

"There's nothing out there," said their father.

The words were barely out of his mouth when the scratching came from the front door.

"What the . . ." Mr. McDaniel reached for the knob.

"No!" shouted Lil and Henry together.

"It's probably just a cat," their father said, ignoring their pleas. He pulled the door open.

Standing before him was a creature like nothing he'd ever seen before. Its clawed hands reached toward him as it hissed.

He slammed the door shut and secured the lock before running toward his bedroom. Lil and Henry stood rooted in horror beside their mother, whose body trembled as she wrapped her arms protectively around their shoulders, never taking her eyes off the door.

Their father returned with a pistol in one hand and a flashlight in the other.

"Henry, hold this light for me," he said, extending the flashlight to his son.

Henry took it, flipped it on, and held it over his father's shoulder as he stood terrified behind his dad.

Mr. McDaniel steadied the gun in his hand and pulled the door open.

The creature stood about 12 feet away from the porch. It turned and looked back at them. Its gray skin seemed to glow in the dim moonlight. Its wide, pink eyes were as bright as the beam of the flashlight.

The creature jumped forward with a hiss, its little arms outstretched and talon-claws scratching at the air. Henry recoiled at the full sight of the creature moving toward them, strangely, on three legs.

Henry's father aimed the pistol and fired. *Bang!*

The creature jumped back with a howl. It leaned forward on its third leg and hissed.

Henry's father fired again.

Bang!

The monster turned and ran, an awkward, loping, hop-run, as two more shots rang out.

The beast disappeared into the darkness. Mr. McDaniel slammed the door shut and turned to his wife. "Call the police," he said, his voice unsteady.

* * *

"Tell me again what the caller said," State Trooper James Masser asked his partner.

His partner laughed loudly. "You heard it right, Jimmy. A three-legged creature with glowing pink eyes tried to get into their house."

"We always get the fun ones," Jim said with a shrug as he pulled into the driveway.

Gravel crunched underneath the car as it made its way toward the house.

"See anything glowing?" asked his partner.

Jim shook his head and laughed as they got out of the car. He adjusted his belt and put his hand on his firearm.

He wasn't afraid of any monster lurking in the shadows, but he'd learned that, in odd calls like this, the caller was probably the one to fear.

Together, the troopers climbed the steps to the front porch. His partner rapped on the door. "Mr. McDaniel," he shouted, "we're here to talk about what you saw."

The door opened, and Mr. McDaniel peered nervously over the men's shoulders, a look of genuine concern on his face. "Come in. We don't want to talk out here." His voice dropped to a whisper. "In case it comes back."

The officers stepped inside. Mrs. McDaniel gestured toward the tidy kitchen. A pistol and flashlight on the table were the only things that seemed out of place. "Come in, officers," she said. "Can I get you some coffee?"

"No, thanks, ma'am," said Jim, taking a small notebook from his pocket. "Do you mind if we ask a few questions?"

Mr. McDaniel sat in a chair beside his wife. In a small living room off the kitchen, Lil and Henry sat on the couch, frozen in place, watching the officers intently.

"Mr. McDaniel, why don't you tell us what happened?" Jim said, still standing.

At the invitation, Mr. McDaniel's words rushed out. "We came home from a meeting. The door was locked. We never lock the door. When the kids let us in, they said a monster was trying to get into the house. I didn't believe them, at first, but then something started scratching at the door. I got my .22, and I shot at it. I know I hit it once, but it ran off."

Jim made notes in his book. "Can you tell me what it looked like?"

"It had gray skin, no fur, and big, pink eyes that glowed like flashlights."

Jim stopped writing and looked up. It took all of his effort not to smile.

"How did you get such a good look at it in the dark?" asked his partner. "Were the eyes *that* bright?"

"I had a flashlight, too."

"About how tall was it?" asked Jim.

"Probably four to five feet."

"Have you been drinking tonight?" asked Jim's partner.

"No," said Mr. McDaniel, the frustration evident in his voice. "We were at a school meeting." He looked at his children. "They saw it, too."

"It was trying to get in through the window with the air conditioner," said Lil. "It had short arms, but it was tall enough to reach the bedroom window."

"And it had three legs," Henry added.

Jim flipped his notebook closed without writing anything else. "Okay, folks, we'll go outside and take a look around."

"Be careful," whispered Lil. "It might still be out there."

"Don't worry, we'll be careful." His partner gave a wink.

They went to the front porch. Mr. McDaniel followed them out the door.

"Look here," Mr. McDaniel said to Jim, "on the door. And here, on the side." He pointed at the deep scratch marks etched in the door and the frame. "It did that."

Jim traced his hand along the deep grooves. "Huh, look at this," he said to his partner.

"Sure looks like something was trying to get in," said his partner.

"Maybe it left some track prints," said Jim. He took his flashlight from his belt. "Which way did you say it went?" he asked Mr. McDaniel.

"Toward the train tracks." Mr. McDaniel pointed into the darkness.

"We'll take a look and be right back," said Jim's partner.

Together, the officers crossed the driveway with Jim's flashlight pointed at the ground. They hadn't gone far when they saw the tracks. Jim bent to study them: two big prints and a single, smaller one just in front.

"Look," he said to his partner with a shiver, "six toes on each. Do you know of any living creature that has six toes? And three legs?"

"No," said his partner. "Maybe they *weren't* making all of this up . . ."

MICHIGAN DOGMAN

Traverse City, Michigan, April 1987

John passed the oncoming car, and then he flipped the brights of his pickup back on and glanced at the dashboard clock. The drive from Traverse City back to his home in Luther shouldn't take too long. He figured he'd be home before midnight.

That song came on the radio again: the one that had started as an April Fools' joke, cooked up by two radio DJs. It had the whole town of Traverse City worked up about a legendary monster dogman. John listened as the song told about the sightings and legends. He couldn't believe the hoax had earned national attention.

The song concluded with these haunting words: "Somewhere in the north woods darkness, a creature walks upright. And the best advice you may ever get is never to go out . . . at night."

John shivered. It was the first time he'd heard the song while driving down a Michigan country road at night. In this setting, it had a disturbing effect.

John was about to change the station when the radio host's voice came on. "Jack O'Malley got an interesting call that came in after he played that song this morning. Stay tuned during this quick commercial break, and we'll play the clip when we come back."

John sighed and decided to keep listening. He suffered through a string of commercials. He'd missed the morning show, and Jack O'Malley was his favorite. But by the time the commercials were done, he'd almost forgotten what he was waiting for—until he heard Jack O'Malley's voice.

"Hello, caller, you're on with O'Malley. What did you want to tell us?"

The wheezy voice of an elderly man answered, "That song chills me to the bone. I saw it. Many years ago, I saw a dogman monster."

O'Malley chuckled. "Thanks for the call, sir. For all you folks listening out there, remember: The legend says the dogman appears every seven years. Keep your eyes open."

John laughed along with O'Malley, and this time he did change the channel.

* * *

Luther, Michigan, July 1987

John went around to the back of the truck and filled his arms with grocery bags, while his wife went ahead to open the front door. He was already on his way, behind her, when he heard her scream.

From inside, their black lab, Chief, started barking.

"What's the matter?" he asked, hurrying to her.

"Look," she said. "Look at all of those marks. Someone was trying to get into the house."

John settled the grocery bags on the porch and studied the marks. The entire doorframe was destroyed, marked with jagged scratches and splintered wood.

"Look. It's over here at the window too." She pointed at the front window.

John studied that spot, too.

"And, gross! It looks like slobber all along here." Even though she hadn't actually touched it, she yanked her hand away from the window as if she had.

"Look at this," John said. He pointed at a tuft of black fur, caught in the splintered wood.

"What do you think it was that did this?" she asked. "A bear, maybe?"

John shuddered. "Bear marks don't look like that. And I can't think of any animal's that do. Maybe it was the dogman monster."

BEAST OF BRAY ROAD

Erin, Wisconsin, November 9, 2006

Nathan had been driving for a while, picking up roadkill along Highway 167. As he cruised through the dark night, he spotted yet another victim: a fairly small deer. He eased onto the shoulder, switched on the flashing light atop his truck and pulled out his list of scheduled pickups.

"Hmm, this guy's not on my list," he said to himself.

He set down the list, grabbed his gloves and then opened his door. Before getting out, he turned on the light in the truck bed. Eyeing the deer, he debated getting the aluminum ramp, which he sometimes used to drag larger carcasses into the truck. This deer was small enough—well under 100 pounds—that he decided he could do without the ramp.

He walked over to the carcass and heaved it up, into his arms. He carried it toward the truck. "You must be a fresh one," he said.

Most of the animals that he gathered were already stiff from rigor mortis setting in, but this one hung limply in his arms. Despite his sturdy frame and the strength he'd developed from doing this work, heaving the dead deer into the back of the truck took a good deal of strength. But Nathan managed.

With the deer in the back, Nathan reminded himself to make note of his unplanned stop. He hurried into the cab and out of the cold November air, leaving the tailgate open. Behind him, the light in the truck bed shone against the bloated bodies of roadkill that he'd gathered.

He was startled when the truck began to shake. It stopped for a moment but then shook again.

"What in the—" Nathan began to say. But he caught movement in his rearview mirror. His eyes widened.

Nathan saw a sight that he'd never seen before: A large, furry bear was leaning over the tailgate and into the back of his truck—trying to grab a bite to eat.

Except, it wasn't a bear. It had black hair and stood tall on its hind legs, but its ears weren't round; they were sharp and pointy. Plus, the creature's long, wolf-like muzzle was bigger than that of a bear.

If it wasn't a bear or a wolf . . . what was it? As Nathan realized that he was looking at a creature he couldn't identify, a wave of panic settled in. He shifted the truck into drive and tore away from the scene. A clang of metal hitting the pavement echoed into the night behind him.

"What the—"

His ramp. The creature had pulled the deer out of the truck, and his aluminum ramp had fallen out with it.

Nathan drove for a few minutes to calm down. He wondered how he was going to explain the missing ramp. He didn't like the idea of telling anyone what he'd seen. After all, he'd lived in this area long enough to know that plenty of people had reported seeing a beast much like the creature he'd just encountered. In fact, so many reports had come in near Elkhorn, Wisconsin, in the '80s and '90s that the sightings had been all over the news. The unusual animal was given the name "Beast of Bray Road" because several of the eyewitness accounts occurred along that road. One of the reporters on the case even wrote an entire book about it after she became convinced that the claims could not be a hoax and that the creature could not logically fall into any previously identified species.

Nathan didn't want any of that media attention, and he sure didn't want the taunting that seemed to come with reporting something like this. Those poor people in Elkhorn had been harassed by reporters and practical jokers for a long time after they came forward. No, Nathan wanted to avoid all of that.

Of course, on the other hand, he couldn't exactly return the truck with a missing ramp—not without explaining why it was gone. Nathan decided to circle back. If he found the ramp, he could just pretend that none of this had ever happened.

When he got to the spot where he'd seen the beast, he stopped and cautiously got out. His stomach knotted as he peered around as quickly as possible. Thankfully, whatever he had seen was gone, along with the deer carcass. Unfortunately, the creature must have dragged away his ramp, along with its catch, because the ramp was nowhere to be found.

Nathan climbed back into his truck and kept on with his rounds for a few more hours, debating whether he should report the incident. He worried that people would make fun of him, but he finally concluded that, based on the immense size of whatever had taken the carcass from his truck bed, it was dangerous. People needed to know that this animal was out there. If it would approach his truck with the light flashing, it could be aggressive enough to harm a person.

As he entered the sheriff's office in West Bend, Nathan felt his face flush with heat. He couldn't explain why he was so embarrassed to be making the report, except that he was a rational person and what he was about to tell the officer on duty seemed a little crazy.

"Can I help you?" the deputy asked politely.

"Yes, sir," Nathan replied, clearing his throat. "I need to report seeing a large animal out on Highway 167."

The deputy raised an eyebrow. "Alright, what exactly did you see?"

"Well, it was big and covered in fur like a bear, but it wasn't a bear." Nathan shifted his weight and swallowed. "If you took a wolf's head and enlarged it and set it on a bear's body, that's what it looked like."

The deputy wrote notes as Nathan spoke. The deputy asked, "Could it have been someone in a fur suit?"

Nathan chuckled nervously. "This was an unscheduled pickup. No one would have known I was going to be in that area."

"Well, maybe one of your buddies thought it'd be fun to scare you," the deputy persisted.

Nathan replied, "It didn't have the size or form of a person. Besides, who'd want to jump into a truck full of roadkill, just for a laugh?"

"Bears are rare around here," the deputy replied, still trying to grasp a logical explanation. "But they do come around, from time to time."

"I've seen all kinds of animals on the side of the road, making dinner out of the carcasses that I'm coming along to pick up. I know what a bear looks like," he protested.

Just as Nathan feared, word quickly got out about his experience on Highway 167. By the next night, it was all over the news. Nathan refused to show his face on camera, and people had begun to say that he'd perhaps seen bigfoot, but Nathan felt certain that the creature was not bigfoot.

After two days of news coverage, another person came forward to say they'd seen the same creature around that area, a couple of years earlier.

* * *

With accounts of this type of beast in the area dating back to 1936, it seems clear that there is something living among the trees and pastures of Wisconsin, something that is elusive enough to avoid capture but not afraid to have close encounters with humans. All witnesses firmly deny that it could be a bear. And although it looks more like a wolf, it walks and even runs on two feet—a physical improbability for a standard wolf. If a wolf wanted to run away, it would naturally do so on four legs, not two.

All of this certainly leaves us to wonder if it could be some sort of werewolf. But without physical evidence, wondering is all we can do.

THE LOVELAND FROGMEN

Cincinnati, Ohio, Spring 2014

Candice caught sight of the green poster, the one with the frog, out of the corner of her eye. She read it, stopping her boyfriend, whose hand she was holding, abruptly beside her.

"It's the Loveland Frogs," she read out loud. "They've gone and made a musical about them."

"Who made a musical about what?" asked her boyfriend.

"Our favorite play from the Fringe Festival," she said. "Remember?"

"Of course," he answered. "Who doesn't love a good spoof of *Ghostbusters*?"

Their favorite show from the 2012 Cincinnati Fringe Festival had been *Don't Cross the Streams: The Cease and Desist Musical* by Mike Hall and Joshua Steele.

"But what's a Loveland Frog?" he asked.

Candice laughed. "I always forget you didn't grow up around here." She led her boyfriend to a nearby bench and pulled her smartphone from her purse. "Well, let me tell you about the legends of the Loveland Frogs." She clicked through her phone to bring up the stories. "Back in 1955," she said, "a businessman was driving late at night and saw three creatures on the side of Hopewell road. They were three to four feet tall, and they stood up straight, on their hind legs. Their hands and feet were webbed, and they had heads and faces like frogs."

"Seriously?"

"It gets better," she said. "One of them held a wand, and it shot a spray of sparks."

Now her boyfriend laughed.

"There's more," said Candice. "The next two sightings were in 1972. Police officers. The first, Ray Shockey, was driving along Riverside, heading into Loveland. He said it was icy, and a creature scurried in front of his car. It was 3 to 4 feet tall, about 50 to 75 pounds, with leathery skin."

Her boyfriend sat back on the bench, listening.

"Two weeks later, another officer, Mark Matthews, said he saw something crouched along the icy road. He stopped because he thought it was roadkill, and he was going to remove it. But when he got out, it hobbled away. He shot at it, but it jumped over the guardrail and disappeared." She paused. "Oh, but it says that Matthews later recanted his story."

Her boyfriend nodded. "If anyone can turn all of that into a good show, it'll be those guys." He studied the details on the poster behind them, and then he pulled his own phone from his pocket. "I'm getting us tickets for opening night. There's no way we can miss this one."

BIGFOOT

BIGFOOT OF TWO HARBORS

Two Harbors, Minnesota, February 1972

It was President's Day weekend, and Kerry Peterson was excited for an extra day off from school. A three-day weekend in northern Minnesota, in February, meant more time to snowmobile. With the sun shining brightly, it was a perfect winter day for being outside, cruising across the trails that bordered the small town of Two Harbors.

With about 24 inches of snow and drifts that were higher in some places, thanks to a recent blizzard, there were lots of great places to take the snowmobile. The Peterson family owned two of them. Kerry bypassed the powerful Arctic Cat, his father's pride and joy, for the smaller Ski-Doo. It had more wear and tear, so that was the one the kids usually rode.

To make the most of his day off, Kerry decided to go back to a place he'd found by accident a few weeks earlier. The area was several miles north of town and was only accessible by riding on a secluded, "secret" trail for quite some distance.

Kerry drove the snowmobile up to the trail and got off his sled. The combination of the snow and the flat, unused trail meant the snowmobile could fly effortlessly over the powdered ground. No matter the terrain or trees on either side, he had a straight, smooth ride.

He headed north for about six miles, until he reached the hidden fields. The land was flat terrain for as far as he could see. He stopped there to check his fuel, wanting to be sure that he'd still make it back to town.

A short while later, he decided that it was time to head for home. Finding the trail again, Kerry began to make his way toward Two Harbors. After about 15 minutes, he entered an area with thick woods on both sides, but his open path ensured him safe passage between the heavy brush. It also gave him a perfect vantage point to see a large figure emerging from the woods.

Kerry thought that it was strange to see anyone out in the middle of nowhere. Yet someone or something walked onto the trail, pushing aside the deep snow like it was nothing. The shape was one color from head to foot: brown, like a chocolate Labrador Retriever.

Curious, Kerry slowed the snowmobile to figure out who—or what—he was looking at. He wondered if perhaps it was a lost hiker or snowshoer. But why would anyone be out here, walking through deep snow?

As he got closer, Kerry saw that the face was a lighter brown around the eyes, nose and mouth. The figure was really tall—taller than anyone Kerry had ever seen.

His part of the trail was too narrow. Kerry couldn't turn around without stopping his snowmobile and dragging it around to face the other direction. He had no choice but to stay his course.

Speeding closer and closer, he tried to think. He didn't know what the creature was or what it might be capable of doing. He flipped on the headlight of the snowmobile, hoping to scare it enough that it might think twice about approaching. Turning its head in Kerry's direction, the monster stopped and watched him for a moment. Then it crossed and disappeared into the woods again.

Shaking with fear, Kerry sped, full-throttle, all the way back into town—never again to return to that remote area of the woods.

To this day, he can't say for sure what exactly the creature was—he never saw anything like it before or since. But no matter how he tries to rationalize his encounter or explain it away, he keeps coming back to one conclusion: He crossed paths with bigfoot.

MOMO (MISSOURI MONSTER)

Louisiana, Missouri, July 11, 1972

"Catch him, Terry," Wally Harrison shouted to his older brother. "We gotta catch him!" Wally's five-year-old legs couldn't run any faster.

The brown dog darted through the trees, out of sight.

"We can't catch that dumb dog. We need to get Doris to come help," said Terry, panting to catch his breath. He dropped to his knees.

Wally plopped down beside him. "Doris!" he yelled.

Terry slugged him on the arm. "She ain't gonna hear us all the way out here. Come on." He tugged at Wally's sleeve and pulled him to his feet.

The boys trudged back toward the house. Before they made it all the way, Terry stopped. He grabbed his little brother's arm, and Wally looked up.

On the other side of the house, near the treeline, stood a tall creature with dark hair covering its face.

The monster held something in its arms. Whatever it was, it was dead and full of blood.

A putrid stench wafted toward the boys, unlike anything they had ever smelled before.

Terry screamed. Wally started to cry.

Neither of them wanted to move, not sure what the thing would do.

Inside, Doris was cleaning the bathroom. She heard the panicked screams of her little brother. She ran to the door, yanked it open and hurried out. She saw a monster holding a dead dog. Dried blood matted the dog's black fur.

"Hurry, come in!" she yelled to her brothers.

At her words, their feet were able to move again. They ran to her and to the safety of the house. The creature gave a loud roar and darted toward the woods.

Terrified, Doris went to find her father.

* * *

Priscilla turned the heat off under her frying pan and set down her spatula. She went into the living room and turned up the volume on the evening news. A local reporter was talking about the most recent development in the Momo case.

She mentally tallied the previous accounts. There'd been a man who reported being chased by a monster with red eyes. Two women on a picnic claimed it chased them to their Volkswagen and only left after they blared the horn. Another got a glimpse of it in his flashlight, and that's not counting the school children who claimed to see it from their classroom window. Just last week, the report had been about the bus that arrived from the West Coast, filled with bigfoot hunters.

Today, though, the reporter talked about footprints. Clyde Penrod showed off the plaster imprint he'd made of the print he'd found. It was huge, with a big heel and three toes. The reporter admired his foresight to preserve the print.

Priscilla shook her head and turned off the television. The bigfoot sightings had put their little riverside town on the national map. The local Dairy Queen had even added a Momoburger to their menu. Momo sure had sparked up their town—but she didn't believe in Momo.

To this day, Priscilla Giltner believes that Momo was a prank by some of her former students. But she refuses to mention any names. The attention that Momo brought to their quiet town was nothing but good.

* * *

Despite being harassed by kids at school because of her sighting, Doris Harrison stands by her experience. She and her brothers reported exactly what they had seen— no more and no less. Doris still doesn't like to talk about the creature, but she knows that Momo was real. She saw and experienced it for herself.

COHOMO (THE COLE HOLLOW ROAD MONSTER)

Pekin, Illinois, May 25, 1972

"I'm telling you: It was about 10 feet tall, covered in dirty white fur, and it made a horrible screeching sound as it walked through the Illinois River." The caller's voice trembled as she spoke. "It was huge, and it smelled awful—worse than an outhouse on a sunny August day."

"Alright, ma'am, we have a deputy in the area looking into the matter," the dispatcher replied.

* * *

"How many of these calls do you suppose we're going to get?" the deputy on duty asked.

"They've been coming in steady all night. I'd say we're way over 100," the dispatcher said. "Thank goodness, I'm about to end my shift."

"That boy out on Cole Hollow Road really set off a firestorm," the deputy noted.

It had been about a week since 18-year-old Randy Emert reported seeing a similar creature while out on Cole Hollow Road with his friends. The boys described the monster as being covered in white fur and standing about 10 feet tall. They thought the creature might be living under an abandoned house not far from where they encountered it.

Since Emert's report, several others in the area had claimed to see the same type of beast. On this particular night, the reports were coming in nonstop.

The radio buzzed. A voice came through. "Still haven't come upon any abominable snowmen out here. Over."

The deputy picked up the receiver and pressed the button. "Well, you've got at least one more to check on. Maybe this will be the one," he replied. "If you find him, tell him he's visiting us during the wrong season. Invite him back in December."

* * *

July 1972

"Alright, fan out people! We're going to search every inch of this area. If there's a bigfoot or any other sort of creature hiding around here, we're going to find him tonight!" James Donahue, the Tazewell County Sheriff declared.

There had been so many reported sightings of the 10-foot-tall beast that the sheriff organized a search party. About 100 people in the community came to help look for the creature they'd started calling Cohomo, short for Cole Hollow Road Monster. Armed with guns, the mass spread out across the countryside.

They scoured the abandoned home where Randy Emert and his friends speculated that the creature might be living, but they found nothing more than a few empty beer cans. Sheriff Donahue doubted that the monster was responsible for leaving those there.

After hours of searching, a shot rang out. Everyone froze. Could it be that someone in the search party had found and shot the creature?

A voice came through the static on Sheriff Donahue's walkie-talkie. "We've got a situation here." The voice paused. "Carl Harris has shot himself in his own dang leg. Over."

Donahue shook his head. "Alright, we'll get a medic over there. It's been a long day; let's call it a night. Over."

* * *

July 28, 1972

"Hello, we're calling to report a Cohomo sighting."

"Tell me what you've seen," the dispatcher replied.

"My wife and I just saw it out in the woods. It was 10 feet tall, with a long face and U-shaped ears. When it opened its mouth to make this awful screeching sound, we saw it had sharp teeth. I'm telling you, it looked like a cross between an ape and a caveman. It even had thumbs!"

"You got close enough to see all that?" the dispatcher asked as she scribbled notes on a pad.

"It wasn't far from us, maybe 20 yards. And the smell was overwhelming, like sulfur."

"We'll have an officer stop by shortly to check things out," the dispatcher replied before ending the call.

Her supervisor looked at the note she'd written. "We actually have an officer in that area now. Someone called in earlier this evening, claiming to see the same thing out that way while picking berries by the old coal mine. She was so afraid, she ran off without her purse."

"And the weirdness continues," the dispatcher replied.

* * *

In 1991, Randy Emert contacted the *Peoria Journal Star*. His was one of the first reports of the Cohomo sightings in Illinois. Randy confessed that he and his friends had made their sighting up, hoping to scare a friend who worked the night shift at a local gas station.

However, there were hundreds of other sightings—too many for Cohomo to have been a hoax. Reports provided similar descriptions and details of the beast, and many of these eyewitness accounts came from reliable and respected local citizens. One sighting even came from an out-of-towner who had never before heard of Cohomo.

After July of 1972, the Cohomo sightings came to an abrupt end. There's little doubt that these people saw something—but what? That question remains a mystery.

TAKU-HE

Little Eagle, South Dakota, Mid-September 1977

The crescent moon hung low in the clear night sky, casting shadows across the field. Chris Hawiatow walked casually, with the two other men following close behind. They had come to check the cattle, as they did every night. They'd lived on the Standing Rock Reservation their whole lives and were familiar with the threats to their livestock. Creatures of all shapes and sizes lurked on the edge of the darkness, waiting for a sign of weakness in one of the cows or for an inattentive mother to let her calf stray too far. Mostly, the men worried about coyotes.

Although a couple of men came armed with rifles, they had little intention of using them to kill. They preferred to shoot warning shots to scare off predators, if necessary, which usually wasn't. This was a time of the day that Chris looked forward to: a moment of general peace, when he could take in the nighttime chirps of crickets and the sparkling Milky Way that could be seen on clear nights, like this one.

The steady sound of crickets aside, all was quiet, except for an occasional cattle hoof smacking against dirt. So when an eerie screech filled the air, the men were noticeably startled. They froze in their tracks.

"Did you hear that?" one of them asked. His long ponytail whipped against his back as he looked from one side of the pasture to the other.

"Yeah," Chris replied, looking around to see where the noise might have come from.

"That wasn't a coyote," another man said, pulling his rifle to his chest.

"I'd agree. That sounded like something in pain, but not a coyote," Chris said.

"What do you suppose . . ." the ponytailed man began, but his words stopped when a large creature appeared from behind the thick line of cottonwoods that ran along the field.

It stood about nine feet tall. Its thick chest was covered in sandy brown fur, and its legs were the size of a grown man's torso. Chris estimated that the beast must have weighed nearly 900 pounds.

"*Taku-He*," Chris said quietly.

Taku-He was what the residents of the reservation had called bigfoot-like creatures for many generations.

The man with the rifle pointed his weapon toward the creature. He wasn't willing to pull the trigger on the beast at that moment, but he wanted to be prepared if it charged toward them.

Chris gazed at the creature in awe. "Jim Douglas said he saw a *Taku-He* dragging a dead deer through his alfalfa field three years ago, just after that mutilated cow was found. Let's see if we can frighten it away."

The men began to walk toward the creature, shouting as they drew closer. The furry beast saw them coming, bellowed loudly, then retreated into the woods.

The men watched it lumber away. The sound of the underbrush cracking beneath its enormous weight grew quieter as the ape-like creature fled deeper into the trees.

"Should we follow it?" the man asked, lowering his rifle.

"No," replied Chris. "What would we do if we caught up with it? We don't want to harm it, but we have to protect the livestock." He paused. "All who've seen the *Taku-He* say it fears man as much as we fear it—maybe more. I think we have scared it away from making our livestock its dinner. But let's stay in the pasture a while longer to make sure it doesn't come back."

The creature did not return that evening or any other as far as Chris could tell. But it would appear to many other residents over the next three months.

* * *

October 13, 1977

Phoebe Little Dog squinted as she looked out the window. She'd heard the same strange screeching sound coming from the pasture that was heard the week before. That time, when she'd looked out the window, she saw the creature right away. Now she squinted into the field, certain the *Taku-He* was out there somewhere. She saw it lumbering across the pasture, sending the cows running in every direction. Covered in thick, sandy fur from head to toe, the monster looked about nine feet tall.

Phoebe ran to the front door, and holding it open with one foot behind her, she reached out and rang the dinner bell attached to the pillar just above the top step.

The bigfoot startled at the sound and then fled into the nearby woods.

"You're not getting one of our cattle for dinner," Phoebe said as she pulled the door shut firmly behind her. She watched through the front window a while longer to be sure the *Taku-He* did not return. She was relieved not to see it again that evening.

* * *

On November 29, 1977, several newspapers, including *The Toledo Blade* and the *St. Petersburg Times*, ran articles about the influx of reported *Taku-He* sightings in Little Eagle. These included 28 such sightings in only three months. Many were reported by well-respected residents in the community, including local law enforcement.

Fearing a creature they'd heard screeching throughout the night in the woodlands around their homes, several area residents moved away, including a local pastor: Rev. Angus Long Elk and his wife. Others armed themselves with rifles or tranquilizer guns, despite authorities asking them to leave their weapons at home.

The reports seemed to indicate that there were three different *Taku-Hes*: Two taller creatures, one with light fur and the other with darker fur, stood between 6 and 9 feet tall and weighed between 600 and 900 pounds. A third, smaller bigfoot was reported to be 6 feet tall, weighing around 400 pounds.

With all the sightings, the general store in town, which was owned by Gary Alexander, became a makeshift bigfoot information center. One local resident, Ed Meller, even set up a recording station in an RV on a property where multiple sightings had occurred.

With so much media coverage, a bigfoot investigator from New York came to Little Eagle to see what he could find. He was confident that with so many sightings of the creature, it could not be a hoax, and based on the descriptions, it could not be a bear or any of the other local wildlife.

Unfortunately, the gentleman from New York left with no tangible evidence. But the sightings continued on until December 5, 1977. After that date, the *Taku-He* reports stopped completely. What happened to the beasts and where they went remain a mystery. But one thing is for certain: Something lived around Little Eagle, something unlike any animal we've scientifically identified. It is one that has lived in folklore for centuries and will most likely continue to do so for generations to come.

MONSTER CREATURES
OF THE WATER

MAYMAYGWASHI
(THE MICHIGAN MERMAN)

Montreal, Quebec, Canada, 1812

Vanant St. Germain sat down at the bar and nodded at the bartender. "One mug, Samuel," he said firmly.

The young man moved swiftly behind the counter, filling a mug until the foam reached the brim before setting it in front of the weathered man looking back at him.

"You did it, huh? You actually went before the Court of the Kings Bench and signed an affidavit claiming you saw that creature?" Samuel asked, shaking his head.

"You're dang right," Vanant said sternly before taking a swig of the beer. "It may have been 30 years ago, but I can still see that thing in my mind like it was yesterday."

Samuel shrugged, "If you say so."

"I do say so," Vanant replied stubbornly. "And you'd be smart to respect things you don't understand."

"You're a crazy old coot, ya know that?" Samuel said as he moved toward a customer at the other end of the bar, leaving Vanant with his mug of brew and his thoughts—thoughts that took him back to that strange day.

* * *

Pie Island, Lake Superior, May 3, 1782

Vanant and his three-man crew had set up camp on Pie Island on Lake Superior. The men, tired from trapping all day, sat around the fire enjoying some much deserved rum. It took the edge off the aching in their backs from portaging so many miles the day before. A kettle warmed over the fire. The woman, their Ojibwa guide, stirred it occasionally.

"I'm going down to check the fish nets," Vanant said.

"Find us a trout or a nice juicy walleye to go with our beans," one of the men said.

"Or a lobster," added another. He tilted his back as he raised a leather canteen to his lips.

"Maybe I'll wrestle a wild boar on the way and bring you back a ham roast," Vanant replied. He reached down and grabbed the skin of rum from the man's hand. Then he took a long swig.

"I do like ham," the man replied.

Vanant laughed as he dropped the container back into the man's lap. "I'll see what I can do."

The fire crackled about 100 yards behind Vanant as he neared the edge of the water. The moon hung high in the clear sky, its light shimmering on the deep, dark water that stretched before him. The stillness of the night made the surface of the lake look like a sheet of dark glass. But something in the moonlight caught Vanant's eye.

About as far in front of Vanant as the camp was behind him, there appeared to be a person bobbing about. Cocking his head to one side, Vanant squinted his eyes.

That form, it wasn't quite a person. It was child-like in stature and appeared to have brown skin that glistened in the moonlight. Curly hair covered its face, and large, dark eyes stared back at Vanant.

Slowly, the thing raised one arm into the air and placed the other on its hip.

Vanant stumbled backward, not believing his own eyes. Although much of the creature's lower half was immersed in the lake, Vanant could see that its hips and upper thighs appeared to belong to a fish.

"Hey! Come see this," Vanant yelled toward the camp. "There's a creature . . ." He ran quickly back to the fire and retrieved his musket.

The others stopped talking to watch his odd behavior, amused expressions on their faces.

"There's a creature," he gasped, "in the water. Part human. Part fish!"

At the look in his eyes, the men stopped laughing.

"*Maymaygwashi*," the Ojibwa woman said in awe, almost to herself.

The others barely noticed. The men hurried after Vanant.

But the woman moved faster, reaching him first.

At the shoreline, Vanant raised his gun to take aim at the creature that still bobbed in the water.

"No," the Ojibwa woman cried. She tugged hard at Vanant's sleeve, throwing off his aim. "You must not shoot the god from water and the lakes!"

Vanant studied the woman, whose hands still clutched desperately to his arm. Then he looked back to the water, just as the creature slipped below the surface. Only a rippling circle remained in its wake.

"What was it?" Vanant whispered.

"*Maymaygwashi*," the woman replied. She released her hands and cast her eyes to the ground. "If you killed it, you would be cursed forever. Just raising your gun at it will cause a terrible storm to strike us." She looked to the sky with worry.

Vanant gazed toward the cloudless sky; it was so clear that the stars sparkled like a layer of fairy dust. He shook his head. Over the years that he'd been trapping and trading, his respect for the Ojibwa had grown. But the idea that the creature was a merman god who would now cause a terrible storm on a perfectly clear night was beyond his ability to believe.

In the early morning hours, the rain rolled in. The heavens echoed with thunder, and the sky was electrified with lightning. The waters of the vast Lake Superior rose so quickly that the trappers and their guide had to rush for higher ground. They hardly had time to rescue their canoes and equipment from the thrashing, rising waves.

They stayed for three days before the rains finally relented and the waters calmed enough for them to leave the island. As they canoed away, Vanant looked back, filled with unease. He surveyed the water for any sign of the merman. He only saw dark water and foam, churned by the water's constant lapping against the rocky ledges.

The image of the creature would be burned in his memory forever. He vowed to never again raise his gun at a *Maymaygwashi*.

BESSIE

Erie Township, Ohio, May 12, 1887

Henry Dusseau tossed a stack of net to the corner and peeked again into the boat's hold. He was pleased with how the day turned out. At midday, he hadn't been sure they'd fill it by sunset, but they'd managed with—he glanced at the dropping sun—about 45 minutes to spare.

"Laurent," Henry called to his brother. "We will make good time, no?"

"The wind is perfect," agreed his brother.

Henry walked to the front and allowed himself a few minutes to appreciate the brilliant red sky. The waves lapped against the sides of the boat, lulling him into his daily trance. He knew that when they reached the shore there would still be much work to do before the day was finished. But this moment, coming in with a full load of flopping, dying fish, was his favorite part. And today, they were even ahead of schedule. Perhaps, they would be among the first to get to the fishery.

"A good day, indeed," he mumbled to himself.

Henry's eyes scanned the approaching shoreline, watching familiar landmarks grow closer. But his eyes caught something that wasn't familiar: something large and monstrous on the beach. It almost seemed to glow in the glint of the setting sun. It was thrashing about.

"Laurent," he pointed. "Do you see?"

Laurent squinted into the sunset. "What is it?"

"I have no idea," said Henry.

"Hurry, let's go and get a closer look."

Laurent laughed. "It's up to the wind how fast we will go. But she seems to be mostly cooperating."

Within minutes, they were much closer—close enough to see that it was a creature of some sort. It was wriggling and squirming like a beached whale.

"Have you seen anything like it before?" asked Laurent. They were almost to the dock.

Henry replied, "It's like a sturgeon but so much bigger."

"Does it . . . does it have arms?" asked Laurent, squinting again. "It does," he answered his own question. He could see the monster's arms thrashing about, waving in the air.

"In all of my years on the water . . ." said Henry.

Laurent pulled the boat into the dock. Henry scrambled to secure the ropes, and Laurent hurried to help.

"What do we do about it?" asked Laurent. "It's not got long to live. Death will come soon."

They stared, unable to take their eyes off the creature.

Suddenly, the creature stopped moving, exhaled one big breath and lay still.

"We need help," said Henry, his eyes fixed on the beast. "It's dying quick, if it hasn't already. Let's find others."

"And rope," said Laurent, "we will need rope."

Together they ran for help. But when they returned, there were only tracks on the beach where it had slid its great mass back into the water.

They also found several large, fish-type scales. Those, they pocketed as proof.

BOZHO

Madison, Wisconsin, Spring 1917

Peter walked along the Lake Mendota beach, near Picnic Point. He liked how the land jutted out into the water and how, at the very end, it made him feel like he was in the middle of the lake. It was where he came to clear his head after a tough day of classes.

It was almost time for final exams. He could get through a few more weeks. He kicked his feet at the rocks on the beach, satisfied by the scuffling sound of the pebbles scattering every which way.

He picked up a bigger rock and threw it into the lake. *Ker-plunk.* He reached for another and then another. He was about to grab his fourth when his eye caught something unusual on the ground.

Picking it up, he held it against the fading sunset to study it. It looked as if it could be a fish scale, round and tough. But it was much too large. He put it in his pocket to show to his professor.

* * *

"What is it?" Peter asked.

"Ah, yes." His professor adjusted his eyeglasses as he studied the thing Peter had found. "I know this. I came here from New England, you know."

"Yes, sir, I know."

His professor liked to talk about his upbringing and education on the East Coast.

"Because of that, I am acquainted with this species."

"What species is it?" Peter asked.

He handed the scale to Peter. "It is from a sea serpent."

* * *

Fall 1917

The fisherman checked his basket. He just needed to find a few more perch, and he'd have enough for a good fish fry that evening. This was his favorite spot; he'd surely get enough here.

He set his basket down on the beach and rolled up his pants, thankful the early autumn water was still warm enough. He moved slowly, taking care not to step on any rocks, and waded out to where the sand dropped off. He cast his line into the water.

He cast a few times, but each time, he came back with nothing. "Where are the fish today? This is usually my lucky spot," he mumbled to himself.

About 100 feet away, a head emerged from the water. It was like a snake with a large mouth and eyes.

The fisherman stared, frozen with fear. When he came to his senses, he scrambled up to the beach. In his haste, he dropped his pole and left it, with his basket.

When he tried to tell his friends what had happened, they laughed. No one believed his story about the monster in the lake.

* * *

Lorraine shifted her hands underneath her chin, taking care not to get a splinter. The autumn sun felt warm on her back.

"I can't believe it's still warm enough to sunbathe," she said happily as she relaxed on the dock.

There was no answer.

Lorraine stole a sideways glance at her new boyfriend. The sight of his back rising up and down in even repetitions told her that he had dosed off. She smiled and closed her eyes. Lorraine couldn't believe she was so lucky to have hooked such a good guy so early in the school year.

She felt a tickle on the bottom of her foot. She looked again at her boyfriend. He was still asleep, so she closed her eyes.

She felt it again. Turning quickly, she saw the head of a creature breaking the surface of the water. It looked like a giant snake—or maybe even the head and neck of a dragon. But its big eyes were friendly, almost laughing.

The monster stuck out its long tongue, and again, it caressed and licked the soles of her feet.

Lorraine screamed and yanked her feet away. Shaking her boyfriend, she woke him.

"What is it?" he asked, jumping up. "What happened?"

"There's something there! In the water!"

They grabbed their towels and, together, ran up the dock and all the way to the frat house.

MINIWASHITU
(THE ICE MONSTER)

Yankton Dakota Plains of North Dakota,
South Dakota and Nebraska, Circa 1920

Charles poured a cup of coffee and gave it to his friend. Ehawee wrapped her hands around it and blew at the hot steam before taking a sip.

Charles returned the pot to the stove and pushed back the curtain to peer outside. Today, it was snowing, but spring wasn't far away.

"This time of year we need to be wary of *Miniwashitu*," Ehawee said.

"*Miniwashitu*?" asked Charles, bringing his own coffee with him to the table.

"Yes, I think that is the monster you want to know about, the creature you called me here to discuss. It is the time of the ice when *Miniwashitu* stirs."

"Yes," said Charles, "the monster . . ." He retrieved a pen and paper and wrote down the name.

"Tell me again," she said. "Why do you want to know about *Miniwashitu*?"

"It's a story I heard," he said, "about a man who saw it. Not very many years ago. I want to know more about it."

"Tell me," asked Ehawee, "what happened to this man you speak of?"

"He died," said Charles. "I want to know if it's because of the legend, but I can't find much about it. That is always when I call you, to tell me about the legends I can't learn about anywhere else."

Ehawee smiled before taking a sip from her mug. Charles knew that smile. She was happy to help him preserve the history of her people's stories.

Charles smiled back. He enjoyed the stories of his American Indian friend, and he knew that the book he was writing was important. After all, he was helping to preserve the rich Dakota history and legends.

"And tell me," she said. "What did they say it looked like?" Her eyes seemed to sparkle as she spoke.

"I'm not sure," said Charles. "Do you know what it looks like?" He set down his coffee cup and prepared to write.

"They say it has a strange form and is covered all over with hair like a buffalo, but it is red in color." She spoke with her eyes closed, in a rhythmic tone, and her body swayed. "It only has one eye, in the middle of its forehead, with a single horn above that. Its back is notched and jagged, like an enormous saw."

Charles nodded, jotting notes on the paper. "What else can you tell me about this creature?" he asked.

Ehawee took a tentative sip of her coffee and leaned forward. "*Miniwashitu* has seldom been seen by humans. Anyone who saw it said it was dreadful. Sometimes, it has been seen in the water, in the middle of the river, a redness shining like a fire. It makes a terrific roaring sound, and it passes through, breaking up the river ice."

Charles continued to write down her words.

"It is said that the monster still lives and that, in the springtime, it moves up river, breaking the ice." Ehawee opened her eyes and took another sip of her coffee. She waited for him to look up. "They say that anyone who sees this creature during the daytime will become crazy soon after. The person will continue, restless and writhing as if in terrible pain, until he is finally relieved by death."

Charles stopped writing and stared.

"You said the man died. Do you know what happened? Did he see *Miniwashitu*?" Ehawee asked.

He nodded. "They say that he saw it. They say that he barely made it home. When he did, he had lost all of his reason and could not speak coherently. Not long after that, he died."

ALKALI LAKE MONSTER

Hay Springs, Nebraska, July 1923

J.A. Johnson and his friends came over the small rise in the ground, approaching Alkali (now Walgren) Lake, and Johnson nearly tripped over his own feet. There was a creature on the shore, just out of the shallow water. It was less than 20 yards away. The animal turned its head toward them, gave a hiss and slunk back into the water.

The friends had been camping near the lake, and although they'd heard the rumors swirling around town about the monster living in the lake, they never expected to see it. Johnson squinted through the falling darkness and shook his head as if to clear his eyesight and refocus the image.

Had he really just seen it: the creature that had been terrorizing tourists, fishermen and farmers for the last three years?

A distinct and unpleasant odor drifted to them.

"Did you see that?" asked one of his friends.

"What's that awful smell?" the other added.

He was sure now that he really had seen it.

They went back to town and told everyone that the creature was still in the lake.

* * *

The reporter read the letter again. "Are you sure you want me to write this?" he asked.

"They've been seeing that thing for three years," said his boss. "And his letter has a solid description, the best anyone has ever given us. Why don't you go out to Hay Springs and talk to him?"

"Yes, sir." The reporter sighed. He hadn't meant to give himself more work, but he supposed it wouldn't hurt to talk to the man. If nothing else, he could see if Mr. Johnson told the same story he'd set forth in the hand-written account that he'd sent to the *Omaha World-Herald.*

It took the reporter a long time to get to Hay Springs and find Mr. J.A. Johnson. With the man's letter in his hand, he knocked on the door.

"Are you Mr. Johnson?" he asked when a man answered.

"Yes, sir," said Mr. Johnson. "What can I do for you?"

"I'm a reporter with the *Herald.* Can I ask you a few questions about the letter you sent us? About the animal you say you saw?"

"Well, sure you can," said Mr. Johnson. "Come in."

The reporter found himself seated in the living room. He perched on the edge of his seat and flipped to a fresh page in his notebook.

"What do you want to know?" asked Mr. Johnson. "I already wrote down everything."

"I just want to clarify a few things."

"Fire away, then."

"Mr. Johnson," said the reporter. "Can you tell me what it looked like?"

"Including its tail and head? It was probably about 40 feet long," he explained. "I would say it was like an alligator, except its head was stubbier, and there seemed to be a projection that was like a horn between its eyes and nostrils."

"Like an alligator, huh?" asked the reporter.

Mr. Johnson had repeated the same description he'd originally written in his letter.

"But it was heavier than an alligator—and not sluggish like an alligator."

The reporter made a few notes. "What color was it?"

"It was a dull gray or brown. But it wasn't that light out, so it was hard to distinguish its color."

"Did it see you?"

"It lifted its head and made this peculiar hissing noise, and then it just disappeared, back into the water."

"Interesting," said the reporter, making another note. "Where do you think it came from?"

"My theory is that there is a subterranean passage from underground, and there are other monsters like it. But they only come up occasionally."

"Uh-huh," said the reporter, flipping his notebook closed. "Thank you for your time, Mr. Johnson. I think I got what I needed."

"Sure thing," said Mr. Johnson. "Is my story really going to be in the *Herald*?"

"It sure is, Mr. Johnson," said the reporter as he left.

* * *

"What are we going to do?" asked the farmer. "It's eating livestock."

The Alliance Anglers' club was holding a special meeting to discuss the mysterious lake creature.

"We've got to do something," said another. "The tourists are complaining to the Hay Springs Chamber of Commerce!

A few of them said they got chased by the lake monster, and the town has to do something to get rid of it."

"It's terrorizing swimmers," said the owner of the restaurant closest to the lake. "If we don't have tourists, we lose business, and times are tough enough as it is. Now that Johnson went off telling his tale to the papers . . ." His voice trailed off.

"We've already formed posses to look for it—twice," said the club's president. "What else can we do?"

"What would we have done if we'd caught it?" asked the farmer. "I went along on that last one, and even if we had found it, Johnson said it was 40 feet long. A shotgun ain't no match for that."

"We've got to do something," the restaurant owner said again.

"What would work on a sea monster?" someone asked.

"Well, my grandaddy was a fisherman out East," said another. "We could get ourselves a whaling gun and maybe a harpoon line."

The others nodded.

"And then organize another posse. And this time, we need a dragnet," said someone else.

The club's president nodded. "All in favor of ordering a whaling gun and harpoon line?" he asked.

"Aye," said the collective voice of the group.

"I'll send in the mail order tomorrow," he answered. "We're going to catch that Alkali Lake monster."

* * *

Despite their best efforts, the townspeople never captured the Alkali Lake monster. All reported sightings of the creature ceased after the 1920s, but the mystery will live on forever in the archives of the *Omaha World-Herald* and in the folklore passed down through the generations.

THE CLAWED GREEN BEAST

Evansville, Indiana, August 21, 1955

"Hello, Louise?" Naomi gripped the phone in one hand and, with the back of the other, dabbed at the sweat dripping from her forehead. "The kids are desperate to get out of this hot house. Care to join us for a swim?" She glanced at her oldest son.

He stood still in the doorframe, waiting for the verdict.

"Okay, that's fine. Yes, good." She kept her words intentionally neutral. She settled the receiver back on the phone hanging from the wall and then turned to her son, careful not to reveal the answer in her expression.

"Well," said Darrell, unable to stand the suspense. "What'd she say?"

Naomi broke into a smile. "We're picking her up in 10 minutes. Get your brother and sister. I'll pack a basket."

He was already out the door to the backyard, hollering for Darwin and Sandra. Within minutes, Naomi was in her suit, and the cooler was packed with soda bottles and tuna fish sandwiches. It was too hot to get into the car, so the children were waiting next to it.

After the family fetched Louise, it was just a short drive to the river. Darrell leaned back against the seat and closed his eyes, letting the wind from the open window whip his hair every which way. Louise's inner tube was stuffed between him and the passenger seat in front of him, and he had to keep shoving it back down. He was glad that his mom knew how to get to the good swimming spots behind the train tracks.

They parked along a stretch of road where the riverbank wasn't too steep and then gathered their gear.

"Mom?" asked Sandra, on the short hike through the brush and trees. "Why do they call it the Ohio River when this side is Indiana and the other side is Kentucky?"

Her mother smiled. "Because," she answered simply.

Darwin rolled his eyes. "You ask that same question every time we come here."

Sandra stuck her tongue out at her brother and shoved past him to be the first to the water.

Not having any of it, he chased after her, grabbing at her ponytail.

"Ow, Mom!" she screamed.

Naomi sighed. She spread the blanket over a shady spot in the rocky, clumpy grass and pointed. "You two sit here. You have to wait until I say you can swim."

Darrell snickered as his brother and sister sat down on the blanket. He set about, searching the shore for a stick that was long enough to poke at the bottom. He liked to know what was down in the water before he started walking around in it.

Darwin inched to the farthest edge of the blanket, and Sandra scooted to the opposite corner, their backs to one another.

Louise stopped to put her things on the blanket. "Your mother deserves better from the two of you," she scolded. "You just remember that she works hard for you."

"Yes ma'am," Darwin mumbled, poking a small stick into the rocky sand.

Sandra nodded and used the back of her hand to wipe at the tears. She obviously didn't like being reprimanded.

"Now, don't cry," said Louise. "It's just so hot. Give her a minute to cool off; we'll have you in the water in no time." She stood and stepped carefully through the brush to place her tube in the weedy water. Gently, she eased her body into it and pushed back from the edge.

Naomi, already in up to her waist, stretched her arms above her head. "This is the life, Louise. We should start our own country club, right here on the riverside."

Both women laughed, and Naomi dove underwater. She took several strokes and came up for air about 15 yards out. Laughing and treading water to stay in place against the current, she shouted to Darrell, "Quit your worrying about what's in the water, and just get in!"

Darrell scowled at his mother, feeling embarrassed in front of Louise.

"Naomi," shouted Louise, "let the other two get in. They've suffered enough in this heat."

"Oh, alright," said Naomi. "Darwin and Sandra, you can get in, but I don't want to hear another peep out of you."

"Yes, ma'am," said Darwin, scrambling off his corner of the blanket.

"Okay, mom," said Sandra, skipping to the water's edge.

Naomi felt something brush against her leg and kicked hard against it. That was the worst part of swimming here: wondering if the river fish might venture this close to the shore. She leaned back in the water and floated on her back, giving whatever it might be wide berth to lumber on to wherever it was going.

Instead, something reached up and gripped her leg. She screamed, and it tugged hard, yanking her underneath the water.

The water swirled around her, and she fought against the panic that comes with not being able to breathe.

The claw-like grasp on her leg tightened, and she went down, closer to the bottom. With her free leg, she kicked hard at whatever it was, trying to push it away and loosen her trapped leg from its claws. Her foot slipped against the creature's slimy, scaly body.

Naomi knew that she was running out of time. She needed a precious breath of air. With one final kick, she thrashed hard, this time adding a punch to the general vicinity of the creature's head, hoping it didn't have teeth.

Her effort was finally enough. Naomi's head broke the surface of the water, and she gasped.

"Mom!" screamed Darrell, rushing toward the water.

"No," yelled Naomi, sputtering and trying to catch her breath. "Don't come in—there's something in here!"

At the panic in her voice, Darrell froze, and his siblings scrambled back, away from the edge of the water.

Louise, struggling to get out of her inner tube, screamed and pointed. "Look out!"

At the same moment, Naomi felt the creature again. Its clawed hand grabbed at her leg, but she propelled her arms in a strong freestyle stroke and kicked her feet before it could lock its grip. She darted through the water, toward the shore.

Not this time, she thought.

By the time Naomi got to shore, Louise had managed to get out of her floating prison and reached to help her up to safety.

Naomi brushed a hand through her matted hair. The shivers racking through her body seemed somewhat ironic on a 96-degree day. She studied the scratches on her leg. Three parallel gashes—two on her shin and one on her calf—ran down from her knee to her ankle. Right in the middle, a palm-print, bluish-green in color and about the size of an apple, seemed to glow in the hot sun.

"What was that?" asked Darwin.

"I have no idea," said Naomi, unable to keep her voice from shaking.

Sandra rushed to her mother. "I thought it was going to eat you," she cried.

* * *

Not long after, the children were back at school when Naomi answered a knock at the door. She peeked through the thin, pink curtain. A man in a suit stood, waiting. She opened the door.

"Can I help you?" she asked.

"Are you Mrs. Darwin Johnson?" asked the man.

"Yes, I'm Naomi Johnson."

He reached into his pocket and pulled out an ID badge. "I'm from the United States Air Force." He held it out.

Naomi glanced at it before he tucked it back into his suit pocket and took out a small notebook and a pen.

"Would you like to come in?" Naomi asked. "The kids will be home from school soon, and I made some lemonade."

"No, but thank you, ma'am." He glanced around, as if looking to see if there were anyone who might overhear. "It's my understanding that you sought medical attention for an incident that happened while swimming on the Ohio River a few weeks ago."

"Well . . . yes," stammered Naomi. "My leg was bleeding badly. There were large scratches. My friend Louise left and called for an ambulance. I told her she was being silly. But they came, and they treated me there. It was nothing, really."

"Louise?" he asked, flipping through the pages of his little book. "Would that be, Mrs. Chris Lambell?"

"Yes," said Naomi.

"And after, did you speak to the newspaper about the river incident?"

Naomi blushed. "Well, yes, the children told everyone, and my daughter, Sandra, has a friend whose father works at the newspaper. It was just a matter of time before he called to ask about it."

He wrote another note.

"Is there . . . is there a problem?"

"No, ma'am." He smiled.

"Are you sure you don't want to come in?" she asked.

"No, I think we're finished." He flashed his smile again. "But from now on, I would like to highly encourage you not to say anything further about this incident."

Naomi's eyes widened in surprise. "Sir?"

"It's a matter of national security, ma'am. Confidential. Please don't discuss it with anyone further."

"Yes, sir," she whispered. "I understand."

He nodded. "Sorry to disturb you. Have a nice day." He tipped his hat and left.

Naomi closed the door and leaned against it. She pressed her fingers against her forehead, as if to massage away a headache. A shiver raced through her body as the realization of the man's words settled upon her.

She looked down, and her hand reached for the mark on her leg. The bluish-green handprint from that terrible day at the river, it still hadn't gone away—no matter how many times she scrubbed at it.

PEPIE

Lake City, Minnesota, Summer 2004

Carl filled his thermos with steaming coffee and made two ham and cheese sandwiches. Next, he went out to the garage and gathered the fishing gear. It was still early, but the humidity hung in the air, promising sweltering temperatures later on.

Even in the driveway, where he was packing the boat, he could hear his daughter's alarm go off with a jarring, repetitive *beep-beep-beep*. After five such "beeps" it stopped, sending the summer morning into a shocked silence. He smiled. Not many fathers could claim daughters who were willing to get up early to spend the day fishing with their dad.

For Carl, there was no better way to spend a hot summer day than out in a fishing boat with his daughter. He went back into the house to get her.

Still rubbing the sleep from her eyes, and with her messy hair tucked into a ball cap, his daughter met him in the kitchen. "Look Dad," she said, holding up her new digital camera. "I'm bringing my birthday present."

"Don't drop it in the lake," he answered.

"Dad, it's got a string," she said, her voice full of the attitude that only 15-year-olds could master.

At the boat launch, Carl's regular fishing buddy shouted across the parking lot. "Ready to catch some crappies?"

"It's always a good day for a fish fry," he answered. "Any word on where they're biting?"

"The guys that just went out said right around here, just south of city point. But last night at the bar, the fellas said they had good luck at center point."

"Center point it is, then," said Carl.

"My thoughts exactly."

Together they slid the boat off his trailer, and the three of them set off for center point.

Halfway there, Carl caught site of something in the water. It looked like a . . . tree? Lake Pepin was actually part of the Mississippi River, so trees and springtime debris were common in the water in the earlier months, but not in August.

"Slow down," said his friend, pointing at the same object. "A tree, I think."

Carl slowed the boat.

"Dad, that's not a tree," said his daughter. "It's moving."

Carl cut the engine, and the boat bobbed up and down with the waves.

"What is it?" he asked.

They were about 75 yards away. The thing seemed to be some sort of creature, moving through the water, bobbing up and down. Carl could only see the front part of the greenish-yellow torso. The humped body was attached to a long neck that stuck out of the water.

His daughter scrambled to the front of the boat and stood on the seat. Clutching the long string tightly in her fist, she steadied the camera and clicked several pictures in a row. She managed to get more than a dozen shots before the creature ducked under the water and disappeared from sight.

"I've been fishing all over the U.S.," said his buddy. "I've seen whales, sharks and all kinds of big fish . . . but I ain't never seen anything like that."

They waited for several minutes, but the lake remained quiet. The creature never reappeared.

* * *

A few days later, Carl's friend called. "You've got to come over and see what I've found. There's all sorts of information about that thing in the lake!"

Carl's daughter insisted on coming along.

When they arrived, Carl's friend hurried them into the dining room. Spread out across the table were several printouts of Lake Pepin monster sightings.

"I think I know what we saw in the lake. Look," said his friend. "This newspaper article from 1871 says that Lake Pepin is 'infested with a marine monster, between the size of an elephant and a rhinoceros,' and it 'moves through the water with great rapidity,'" he read.

Carl chuckled. "Really?"

He picked up another page and read a different article, this one from 1875. It told about a man and two young boys, on a skiff, going from Lake City to Wacouta. They noticed something strange rise over six feet out of the water before descending back down.

"Those are both older articles," said his friend. "But look here: These are more recent." He handed Carl a stack of photocopies. One from 1987 showed a photograph with what appeared to be a long neck, extending out of the water. The headline read, "Proof Positive."

Carl's daughter pulled her digital camera from her pocket. "Just wait until you see these," she said, her face beaming with a smile. She passed the camera to her dad.

Carl and his friend huddled over it. They flipped through the pictures she'd taken during their day on the lake.

"Holy cow, I think you got him in this one!" his friend said, pointing at the screen.

Carl peered at it closely. "I really think we saw Pepie."

THE MONSTERS OF DEVIL'S LAKE

Sauk County, Wisconsin, October 2015

Sam jammed the last stake into the ground and double-checked his handiwork. His tent was secure, and if the rain that was forecasted for the evening did come, he would hopefully stay dry. He tossed his pack and sleeping bag into the corner and went to find his group of 11-year-olds.

He had been to this park for the Scouting Jamboree many times, and he knew the routine, the activities and the trails pretty well. But this was his first time as one of the teenage group leaders. Even though there were parent chaperones, he'd still be in charge of a group. Complaints had been made about kids misbehaving, so the leaders were under a lot of pressure to make sure this year was better. He was more than a little nervous about keeping a group of younger kids entertained—and behaving—for the next 24 hours. Especially if it rained.

* * *

They had just come back to the tents to retrieve their flashlights and jackets for the bonfire when the first big drops fell. The clouds had moved in, fast and furious, and Sam barely had time to unzip the zipper and herd everyone under cover before it began to pour.

Now, Sam sat, facing a circle of six messy faces, all squished into his four-person tent. It had always seemed spacious in here, until now.

Connor and Max played Rock, Paper, Scissors together. Sam knew from the day's previous events that, if they continued, they'd soon be punching each other. Three of the other kids could hardly sit still, wiggling in their seats, shaking the nylon fabric of the tent. Jasper sat as far on the edge of the group as the cramped space allowed. Sam recognized his own introverted tendencies in this kid and had been trying to include him in activities all day.

A loud noise ripped through the air, followed by the tell-tale smell.

"Oh, Jack, did you have to? I can't believe you farted in Sam's tent!" one of the boys exclaimed.

Everyone snickered. Connor punched at Max.

Sam sighed. He knew that if he didn't think of something quickly, he—and his tent—would probably explode.

"Does anyone know what's lurking out there in the lake?" asked Sam.

Max froze, mid-punch, and said, "I don't know, fish?" He rolled his eyes and laughed.

Everyone else laughed, too, except for Sam and Jasper.

"Do fish have eight legs?" Sam asked. He switched his flashlight on.

"Octopuses don't live in lakes," said Connor and went back to punching at Max.

"Well, there's one that lives here." Sam dropped his voice to a near whisper, forcing the boys to lean in close. He held his flashlight under his chin. "A long time ago, the Native American Indians were scared of this lake—and for a good reason."

He glanced at his charges. He had their attention.

"On a dark, moonlit night, many years ago, a band of Native American men gathered together and headed out on the lake in their canoes. The air was still and silent, except for the sound of the men's paddles cutting gently through the dark water."

Sam realized that all the boys were listening intently. "They paddled slowly and quietly through the lake, with only the light of the moon to guide them."

The rain outside drummed against the tent, a perfect accompaniment to his story.

"In a frenzied flash, tentacles shot out from the lake, flipping over the canoes. The men within them spilled into the blackened ripples of the water. In horror, the warriors' arms flailed around, striking out at the fleshy limbs of the unknown beast that attacked them. The men fought, terrified."

The 11-year-olds shared a collective gasp.

"Alerted by shouts of terror and panicked splashing, the nearby tribe members ran to the lake, where they watched in helpless horror. Their own sobs rose up to meet the screams of the hunters."

"They couldn't do anything?" asked Max.

"Nothing," said Sam. "They could only watch as their Indian brothers were pulled apart by giant octopus arms."

"Then what happened?" someone asked.

"After that, every year, the surviving hunters of the tribe would offer a sacrifice to the demon creature in the lake by throwing animals and gifts to it."

"They don't still do that," whispered Max. "Do they? That means the monster is gone, right?"

Sam nodded. "Maybe, but you should be careful if you decide to go swimming."

Connor buried his head in his hands.

"I'm glad it's too cold to swim," said Jasper.

"Tell us another," said Max.

Outside, the rain continued to beat against the nylon tent. The boys hugged their legs and waited.

"Well, there is actually another story," said Sam. "But I don't know if you can handle it."

"Yes, we can! Tell us!"

Sam sighed, as if he was reluctant to speak. But, really, he was wondering how long he could make this story last. "Okay, but only if you're sure."

"Yes!"

"Okay. Many years later, the Dakota Indian tribe told other stories of a creature in the lake."

"What?" asked Max. "About the octopus?"

"No, this creature was more like a giant fish. A terrible drought struck the area, causing the lake to become very small," Sam said. "One day, the natives saw a creature stuck in the mud. Its large body writhed helplessly. As it wiggled and tried to free itself, its head bobbled on its long neck with each desperate lurch."

"Did they kill it?" asked Max.

"No, they feared killing the creature might put a terrible curse on them," explained Sam. "So they left it alone."

"Did it die?" asked Jasper.

"No, all of that wiggling eventually paid off for the poor fellow, and he managed to squirm his way out of the mud and back into the water."

"That one wasn't scary at all," said Max.

"It is if they never found it and it's still in the lake," said Connor nervously.

Sam shrugged. "If that one's not scary enough, I could tell you about bigfoot."

"Yes," said Max. "I want to hear about bigfoot!"

"They've got a bigfoot around here, too?" Connor asked with a gulp.

Sam realized the rain outside had stopped. "We'll save bigfoot for another time," he said, unzipping the tent and herding everyone out. "The dads made a bonfire, and I'm sure there are marshmallows to cook."

The boys scrambled out into the muddy campground, laughing and cheering; even Jasper joined in.

Sam secured his tent and followed them down the trail. He wasn't surprised when Connor hung back, just to make sure that Sam was coming.

MONSTER CREATURES OF THE AIR

THE VAN METER MYSTERY

Van Meter, Iowa, September 29, 1903

The little girl sat on the porch steps and strained her ears to hear what the grown-ups were talking about inside. She'd been putting together the bits and pieces all day. Last night, or rather, early this morning, when Mr. Griffith was finally coming home, he'd seen a thing. With wings. And a light. It hopped from one building to the next, right in front of his eyes. What sort of monster came with a light, as if it had its own built-in lantern?

* * *

Doctor Alcott had settled himself into bed in his room behind the office where he saw his patients. Lulled by the soft rain, he drifted into a deep sleep. But he was startled awake. A bright light flashed through the window and shone in his eyes. He leapt out of bed, and his hand reached for his gun. He ran outside to see what was going on. All the while, he tried to think of something that would account for the light. There was nothing.

And then he saw it. It was some sort of a creature, not entirely human but not like any animal he had ever known. In the center of the creature's forehead was a single blunt horn. The light appeared to be coming from the horn.

Dr. Alcott grasped his weapon and fired. He hit the beast, yet nothing happened. He fired again and again and again, until he only had one shot left. Not wanting to waste it, he fled back to his office and locked himself inside. He was left to face the night alone, knowing that some indestructible creature was out there. Waiting.

* * *

September 30, 1903

The little girl walked slowly down the street. The grown-ups were whispering again today. Even more than yesterday. Something else must have happened.

She clutched the list in her hand and went into the grocery store. The grown-ups in there stopped talking. While the clerk measured out the flour, the little girl observed the silence. Maybe if she pretended that she were invisible, they'd start talking again, but they didn't.

She counted out the coins and said her thank you.

"Do you really think it could be robbers?" asked one man to another as she walked out the door.

Just before the door shut all the way, she heard the other answer, "I don't know. Whatever it is, it ain't good."

* * *

Peter Dunn said goodnight to his family and pulled the door shut, instructing his wife to lock it behind him. He shifted his shotgun so it rested on his shoulder. He was comforted by the weight of it as he walked. He let himself into the Van Meter Bank, where he was employed as a cashier, and settled in for a night's watch. If there were robbers descending upon Van Meter, he was going to make sure they didn't get into the bank.

At midnight, he counted out the 12 chimes of the town clock. He began to wonder if his night watch duties were necessary. An hour later, the clock clanged once. A strange noise followed. A gurgling of sorts.

His senses were at attention. His skin prickled, and the hair on his arms stood up in salute. Before he could investigate further, a bright light shone through the front window, trapping him in a spot of light. It wasn't until the beam of light moved away that he was able to see a large beast. The light swept back again. Peter aimed and fired at the monster. The glass in the window crashed all around. The creature just disappeared.

When morning dawned, Peter searched outside, expecting—hoping—to find a dead or wounded beast. Instead, all that he saw were the giant tracks of a three-toed creature. He vowed to make a plaster cast of one of them, as proof.

* * *

October 1, 1903

The little girl skipped down the street. She stopped suddenly when she got to the bank. The front window was missing, and Mr. Dunn was sweeping up broken glass.

"What happened?" she asked.

He paused in his task and looked at the girl. "Nothing," he said. "Just an accident. There's nothing to worry about."

The girl studied him as if she wasn't sure whether she should believe him or not.

Peter went back to sweeping the glass.

* * *

Late that night, O.V. White was asleep in his room over the hardware store. He was startled awake by a strange sound, like a wood file rubbing against another.

Grabbing his gun, he darted to the window. He threw it open and peered out into the rainy darkness. As his eyes adjusted, he saw a dark figure. It was perched on the cross arm of the telephone pole, about 15 feet away. But it didn't have the light that the others had talked about.

He aimed carefully and fired. Instead of killing it, he only seemed to wake the monster. It turned on its light and studied him. A strange, awful odor overtook him, and he felt like he was being held in some sort of trance.

* * *

Sidney Gregg was asleep in his store when he was startled awake by a gunshot that came from across the street. He rushed to the door and stared at the creature descending from the telephone pole.

Using its large beak in the same way a caged bird climbs around, it made its way down the pole. When it got to the ground, it flapped its featherless wings. It was at least eight feet tall, and the light on its head was as bright as an electric bulb. The creature flapped its wings again and hopped up and down.

As it did at the same time every night, the mail train passed through town. The sudden noise seemed to surprise the monster, and it flew away, in the direction of the coal mine.

* * *

Late-night October 2, 1903

The little girl was startled awake in the middle of the night by a pounding on the door. She heard her father go to answer it and crept to the hallway to listen.

"Hurry, we've found it," said the man's voice. "Platt, from the brick plant, saw it come out of the old coal mine. There's two of them. Bring your gun; we're going to wait for them to come back. And tell your wife to leave the lights on. Everyone is leaving their electric lights on for the rest of the night."

Without another word, the girl's father turned on the lights in the living room and kitchen. He grabbed his coat and hat and shotgun and followed the man out the door.

The little girl's mother took the girl's hand and settled her back into her warm, safe bed. But the little girl couldn't sleep. She could only think about creatures with wings and light-horns on their heads.

After tossing and turning, her nose smelled coffee and breakfast, the tell-tale signs of morning. She heard her father come in. Again, she crept to the hallway to listen.

"We waited all night," he said to his wife. "At dawn, they finally came back. I've got to tell you, I've never heard so much shooting. The whole town seemed to be shooting at them. But they just looked at us and descended down into the mine."

The little girl heard her mother gasp.

"Don't worry," her father hurried to continue. "I came back to get my shovel. We're going to seal them in."

Feeling brave enough to go into the kitchen, she stood in the doorway, her bare feet cold on the floor.

"Come," said her mother, patting the spot at the table next to where her father sat. He swallowed the last of his coffee and stood. He patted his daughter on the head and kissed his wife on the cheek.

"Don't worry," he said again. "Those monsters aren't welcome in Van Meter, and we're going to make sure they don't come back."

* * *

The townspeople barricaded the entrance to the mine, and the two winged-creatures were never seen again.

THE DEMON LEAPER

Louisville, Kentucky, Circa 1930

Eight-year-old Mary walked into the kitchen of her family's row house on St. Catherine Street and sat beside her great-grandmother. The woman had lived in the house most of her life. It was down from the Gothic Walnut Street Baptist Church, at the corner of Third and St. Catherine, and had been passed down through the generations.

"Grandmother, tell me again about the bat monster," Mary said, her eyes large with excitement. Although the stories frightened her, she still loved to hear them.

"I recall one evening I saw it while I sat on the porch. It was a warm night, and the stars were extra bright. I could see the church very clearly. Oh, the neighbors were so angry about that church! It outgrew its space on Walnut Street, so it set its sights on our neighborhood. But it didn't stop with its purchased lot. The church bought up all the land around it and, without any care or concern for the neighbors, built their front door right up to the sidewalk! All those mansion owners were so angry," she repeated.

"Yes, but tell me about the creature," said Mary.

Sometimes, her great-grandmother got sidetracked.

Grandmother paused to take a sip of tea. She pushed a small plate filled with cookies toward Mary. "Have one. Have two . . . I won't tell."

Mary smiled and took a cookie in each hand.

"I heard it before I saw it. It was like someone shaking out a sheet before they hang it on the clothes line to dry. I'd seen that creature many times before, so I wasn't surprised to look up at the tall steeple and see it hopping around on the roof of the church, next to the gargoyles. He would always set his talons on the rooftop then give his huge, black, bat-like wings a mighty flap, and he'd rise before setting down again."

"Was it as big as Grandaddy?" Mary asked.

"Even bigger," Grandmother replied. "And it also had a horrible hooked beak."

"What'd you do?"

"I hightailed it into the house," Grandmother replied. "I wasn't sticking around to say hello to that thing."

* * *

Approximately 1981

Sam waited for his girlfriend to finish getting ready. She'd come home from her waitress shift at the country club, and they were going to meet friends for the last hours of the night at a nearby bar.

Sam wandered through her gorgeous apartment. His was more convenient for late-night studying and early morning classes because it was closer to the University of Louisville, but hers was definitely cooler. It took up half of the floor of a second-story mansion on Third Street, in a part of town known as Old Louisville.

The whole neighborhood consisted mostly of mansions built in the late 1800s for the city's opulent elite. Now, most of the once single-family homes had been split into apartments, thereby sharing their historical wealth with the masses.

Filled with character and just oozing with charm, his girlfriend's apartment even had a little balcony, only big enough for two tiny lawnchairs. Having to crawl out the window to get to it only added to its eclectic appeal.

Scratch, scratch, scratch. A noise sounded like it was coming from the attic . . . or maybe the roof.

Sam went to the window to see what might be causing the sound. Peering through the curtains, he noticed something perched on the balcony.

His heart skipped a beat.

The thing was huge, much too big to be a bird. The bright streetlight illuminated the dark figure as it stood and stretched out its bat-like wings, which must have been around 10 feet wide.

Sam wondered, rather seriously for a minute, if one of the gargoyles from the Walnut Street Baptist Church rooftop had come to life.

Before he could study it further, the monster jumped into the air. Sam could see its bird-like feet, complete with sharp talons.

"We should go," his girlfriend shouted from the front of her apartment.

Her voice distracted Sam's gaze from the window. When he looked back, the winged creature was gone.

"Yeah . . . let's go," he said.

Once outside, he quickly led her away from the front of the house, where he'd seen the thing.

When they returned an hour later, he couldn't get into the house fast enough.

"What's wrong with you?" asked his girlfriend. "You've been looking over your shoulder all night!"

"Nothing," he answered. How could he ever explain that he'd seen a large bat-bird creature on her balcony?

Through the night, he convinced himself that his mind had been playing tricks on him. But the next day, Sam ventured onto the balcony.

There were massive, scratched imprints in the railing where he'd seen the thing—evidence that something large had been there. He shook his head in amazement. He didn't believe in ghosts and inexplicable phenomena. But something unexplainable had definitely landed on that balcony. His brain couldn't dispute the tangible proof in front of him.

* * *

The Louisville Demon Leaper sightings span decades, yet the description is always the same. Is there something lurking about the Gothic church steeple at the Walnut Baptist Church in Old Louisville?

THE THUNDERBIRD ATTACKS

Lawndale, Illinois, July 25, 1977

"Throw it over here!" ten-year-old Marlon Lowe yelled to his friend. He jumped up and down, waving his hands above his head.

Another friend joined in, waving his arms across the yard. "No, over here!" he yelled.

The three boys had been playing in the backyard for most of the evening while their parents were in the front yard, visiting with their adult guests.

Before Marlon's friend could throw the ball to either of the boys, a shadow darkened the grass around their feet, and the air pulsed with the drum of flapping wings.

The boys looked toward the sky, and their mouths dropped open. Two enormous birds flew toward them.

"What are those?" one of the boys asked.

"I . . . I don't know," Marlon replied.

"They're birds," the other boy said, observing their enormous, black, feathered bodies and the white rings around their necks that led up to seemingly featherless heads. "And they're coming toward us!"

Marlon felt rooted to the ground beneath him as the giant birds came closer and swooped toward his friend, who ran screaming and dove into the nearby pool.

Rising back into the sky, the birds circled the house once before setting their sights on Marlon. Seeing the creatures approaching him, Marlon turned to run but only got a couple of feet before one of the beasts grabbed him by his shirt and lifted him into the air.

Marlon screamed, thrashing his arms and legs wildly.

Marlon's parents, Ruth and Jake, heard the yelling. They looked over to see their son dangling two feet above the Earth, gripped by the talons of a huge, feathered creature.

"Marlon!" Ruth screamed. She ran toward her son, whose legs kicked wildly.

"Holy hell," Jake shouted as he rushed after his wife.

Their friends, Jim and Betty, hurried behind them as Ruth sprinted across the yard after her boy.

"Marlon! Keep hitting it!" she screamed as she gained on the animal, which seemed slightly stunned by Marlon's fists beating at its legs.

The second bird flew beside the one carrying Marlon, who had somehow become their prey.

Jake was on Ruth's heals screaming, "Let him go!"

After flying for a distance of about 40 feet, the bird dropped Marlon. He landed with a thud, and his mother crumbled to the ground, holding the boy in her trembling arms. She looked to the sky, afraid that the birds might return and attack again.

Luckily, the birds seemed finished with their attempt, and with an eerie thrust of their enormous wings, they glided away. The birds disappeared behind the thick trees that surrounded Kickapoo Creek.

* * *

Ruth sat at the wooden table with the large book closed in front of her. The library was quiet, as libraries tend to be, except for the few hushed whispers from those who seemed more interested in seeing what she was doing than reading the books they'd come to check out. Word had traveled about the incident with the creature the other day, and it seemed that most people thought her family had lost their minds.

Ruth returned her attention to the book in front of her, flipped open the cover and gazed down the index page. Then she began paging through the book slowly. She inspected the illustrations and photographs of birds and bird-like creatures.

Jake dropped into the chair beside her, carrying a stack of books in his arms. "If no one will believe us, we need to figure out what this is on our own," he said.

He had been unable to hide his frustration over the police doubting what his family had seen, when called to their home following the attempted abduction of their son. Even with Jim and Betty there to back them up, the police openly called them liars.

And worse, night after night, Marlon suffered from nightmares about his terrifying experience. Of course, he wasn't alone. Jake would never shake the image—or the helplessness he felt watching his son get carried away by a giant bird.

Before Jake could open any of the books he had lugged over, Ruth grabbed his arm. Never looking away from the book in front of her, she said, "I found it."

Her book was opened to a page featuring a large photograph of a condor. It looked exactly like the birds they'd seen in their yard.

* * *

Between Armington and Delavan, Illinois, July 29, 1977

Not more than 20 miles from where Marlon was lifted off the ground by an immense bird, local mail carrier James Majors was completing his early morning deliveries. It was around 5:30 a.m.

He'd heard others talking about the large birds that had been spotted during the week around the area. One woman near Armington had reported seeing a bird that she claimed was "larger than the hood of her car," only yesterday. Then a couple hours later, a family had seen the same sort of creature land on the roof of their barn while they were out flying model airplanes.

James wasn't sure what he made of all the talk about the beastly creatures that locals were calling Thunderbirds. They seemed like something from a prehistoric time, and he wasn't one to believe in nonsense like bigfoot and the Loch Ness Monster.

As he delivered a bundle of letters into a mailbox he'd stopped beside, he caught sight of something through his windshield. Across the road, hovering over a cornfield, two large birds circled in the air.

One of the creatures swooped down and snatched a small pig from the field with its talons. The bird, clutching its squirming prey, flew across the road.

"Holy Mother of God," James muttered, not sure he could believe his own eyes.

The bird's enormous wings flapped above him; the sound pulsated in his ears.

"That sounds like a jet taking off!"

The bird met up with its companion, the pig still dangling from its clutches. Together, the Thunderbirds flew toward the horizon.

* * *

Multiple sightings of what seemed to be a pair of enormous condor-like birds were reported, including a detailed sighting in Odin, Illinois, just a little more than a week later. (A husband and wife described the bird as "prehistoric" with a featherless head and giant wings.) Yet it is unclear exactly what these feathered beasts were and what ever became of them.

If these were some sort of overgrown condors, one has to wonder what brought them to Illinois, far beyond their typical habitat. And since condors can live for 70 years or more, it's possible these child-hungry birds of prey are still out there . . . hunting.

BIBLIOGRAPHY

THE WENDIGO

Crawford, Suzanne J. and Dennis F. Kelley (editors). *American Indian Religious Traditions: An Encyclopedia.* Santa Barbara, CA: ABC-CLIO, Inc., 2005.

Ghosts of the Prairie. "The Wendigo: The North Woods of Minnesota." www.prairieghosts.com/wendigo.html (accessed February 28, 2016).

Lewis, Chad. *The Minnesota Road Guide to Mysterious Creatures.* Eau Claire, WI: On the Road Publications, 2011.

BENTON COUNTY MONSTER SNAKE

Phantoms & Monsters. "Indiana's Monster Snake," October 28, 2013. www.phantomsandmonsters.com/2013/10/indianas-monster-snakes.html (accessed February 14, 2016).

THE VAMPIRE OF NEBRASKA

Bacon, Dale (posted by David Bristow). "Vampires of Nebraska." Nebraska State Historical Society Blog, October 26, 2011. www.blog-nebraskahistory.org/2011/10/vampires-of-nebraska (accessed February 19, 2016).

Wishart, David J. (editor). "Cowboy Culture." Encyclopedia of the Great Plains. http://plainshumanities.unl.edu/encyclopedia/doc/egp.ii.015 (accessed February 20, 2016).

THE MELONHEADS

Creepy Cleveland: Folklore, Myths and Monsters in Northern Ohio. "MelonHeads in Kirtland, Ohio," February 21, 2008. www.creepycleveland.net/2008/02/melonheads-in-kirtland-ohio_21.html (accessed April 6, 2016).

Fox 8 Cleveland. "Urban Legend or Truth? Tale of the Melon Heads in Kirtland," October 31, 2014. http://fox8.com/2014/10/31/urban-legend-or-truth-tale-of-the-melon-heads-in-kirtland/ (accessed April 6, 2016).

Weird U.S. "Melon Heads Creep Through the Ohio Woods at Night." http://weirdus.com/states/ohio/fabled_people_and_places/melonheads/index.php (accessed April 6, 2016).

THE ENFIELD HORROR

Darkes, Chris. "The Enfield Monster Case Study." Shoe Factory Road, July 31, 2015. http://www.shoefactoryroad.com/2015/07/the-enfield-monster-case-study (accessed February 20, 2016).

Montgomery, Dennis. "A Monster at Enfield." *Mt. Vernon Register-News*, April 27, 1973. www.newspapers.com/newspage/30409597/ (accessed February 22, 2016).

MICHIGAN DOGMAN

Charmoli, Rick. "Was the Dogman Responsible?" *Cadillac News*, October 31, 2007. http://www.cadillacnews.com/story/?contId=59088 (accessed March 7, 2016).

Creepypasta Wiki. "The Legend of Michigan's Dogman." http://creepypasta.wikia.com/wiki/The_Legend_of_Michigan%27s_Dogman (accessed March 7, 2016).

THE BEAST OF BRAY ROAD

Faytus, Len. "The Beast of Bray Road's First Appearance." *FATE Magazine: True Reports of the Strange and Unknown*. www.fatemag.com/the-beast-of-bray-road (accessed April 6, 2016).

Godfrey, Linda. "Sightings Log." The Beast of Bray Road: Hunting the American Werewolf, November 10, 2006. http://www.beastofbrayroad.com/sightingslog.html (accessed April 6, 2016).

Papst, Chris. "Special Assignment: Wisconsin Wearwolf." WMTV NBC 15, November 13, 2009. www.nbc15.com/home/headlines/70005732.html (accessed June 17, 2017).

THE LOVELAND FROGMEN

Behind the Curtain. "Hot Damn! It's the Loveland Frog Review," May 30, 2014. https://behindthecurtaincincy.com/2014/05/30/hot-damn-its-the-loveland-frog-review (accessed June 15, 2016).

Creepy Cincinnati. "The Loveland Frogmen," October 3, 2014. www.creepycincinnati.com/2014/10/03/the-loveland-frogmen (accessed June 21, 2016).

Gasden Times. "Loveland Frog," October 18, 1985. https://news.google.com/newspapers?nid=1891&dat=19851018&id=trgfAAAAIBAJ&sjid=stcEAAAAIBAJ&pg=4397,2803271&hl=en (accessed April 7, 2016).

Lee, Marika. "'Loveland Frogmen' Gets Own Musical." *Cincinnati Enquirer,* May 22, 2014. www.cincinnati.com/story/news/local/loveland/2014/05/22/loveland-frog-gets-musical/9455233 (accessed April 7, 2016).

Morphy, Rob. "Loveland Frog Men: (Ohio, USA)." Cyrptopia: Exploring the Hidden World, December 16, 2009. www.cryptopia.us/site/2009/12/loveland-frog-men-ohio-usa (accessed June 21, 2016).

THE DOGMAN OF KANSAS

Dogman Field Research Organisation. "Dogman Sighting Outside Lawrence Kansas," June 30, 2014. http://www.dogmanresearch.com/2014/06/dogman-sighting-lawrence-kansas.html (accessed April 13, 2016).

BIGFOOT OF TWO HARBORS

Interview with Kerry Peterson, April 3, 2016.

MOMO

Columbia Daily Tribune. "Town recalls 'Momo' saga," July 15, 2012; updated January 29, 2013, www.columbiatribune.com/wire/town-recalls-momo-saga/article_294d359b-0519-51af-bdba-8d70cfa87859.html (accessed April 11, 2016).

Hart, Rodney. "Remembering Momo: Stories about creature 40 years ago give spark to quiet little Mississippi River town." *Herald-Whig*, July 11, 2012; updated July 25, 2012. www.whig.com/story/18997927/remembering-momo-stories-about-creature-40-years-ago-give-spark-to-quiet-little-mississippi-river-town# (accessed April 11, 2016).

COHOMO (THE COLE HOLLOW ROAD MONSTER)

Coleman, Loren. "Cohomo Monster: 1972." Cryptomundo, November 6, 2006. http://cryptomundo.com/cryptozoo-news/cohomo-1972 (accessed March 29, 2016).

Pekin Daily Times. "Hey, Bud, Did You See A Monster Go By…" July 27, 1972 (accessed via www.bfro.net/gdb/show_article.asp?id=631 on June 22, 2016).

Vogel, Nick for the *Pekin Daily Times*. "Did a hairy monster stalk Tazewell County, Illinois?" Bigfoot Encounters. www.bigfootencounters.com/articles/tazewell_county.htm (accessed March 29, 2016).

TAKU-HE

Toledo Blade. "Indians Move Off Reservation As Bigfoot Moves In," November 29, 1977. https://news.google.com/newspapers?nid=1350&dat=19771129&id=HQ9PAAAAIBAJ&sjid=YwIEAAAAIBAJ&pg=2257,1589189&hl=en (accessed March 29, 2016).

MAYMAYGWASHI

French Wikipedia. "Maymaygwashi." http://wikipedia.qwika.com/fr2en/Maymaygwashi (accessed February 8, 2016).

Michigan's Other Side: Exploring the Strange & Unusual in the Great Lakes State. "The Michigan Merman." http://michigansotherside.com/the-michigan-merman (accessed January 24, 2016).

Phillips, Jim. "A Brief History of the King's Court Bench for Upper Canada, 1791–1841." The Osgoode Society for Canadian Legal History. www.osgoodesociety.ca/encyclopedia/a-brief-history-of-the-court-of-kings-bench-for-upper-canada-1791-1841 (accessed February 2, 2016).

Wisconsin State Journal. "Odd Wisconsin: The Merman of Lake Superior," November 17, 2009. http://host.madison.com/wsj/news/local/odd-wisconsin-the-merman-of-lake-superior/article_7b4451ac-d3a2-11de-949b-001cc4c03286.html (accessed January 24, 2016).

BESSIE

Bogue, Margaret Beattie. *Fishing the Great Lakes: An Environmental History, 1783–1933.* Madison: The University of Wisconsin Press, 2000.

History of Ottawa County, Ohio and its Families, The. Oak Harbor, OH: The Ottawa County Genealogical Society, 1985 (accessed via http://carrolltownship.net/history.php on February 26, 2016).

Ho, Oliver. *Mutants & Monsters (Mysteries Unwrapped).* New York: Sterling Publishing Company, Inc., 2008.

New York Times, The. "A Fresh Water Sea Serpent," May 14, 1887. http://query.nytimes.com/mem/archivefree/pdf?res=9807E1DE17 30E633A25757C1A9639C94669FD7CF (accessed February 26, 2016).

BOZHO

Brown, Charles E. "Sea Serpents: Wisconsin Occurrences of These Weird Water Monsters In the Four Lakes, Rock, Red Cedar, Koshkonong, Geneva, Elkhart, Michigan and Other Lakes." Madison, WI, 1942 (accessed via www.wisconsinhistory.org/turningpoints/search.asp?id=1622 on March 4, 2016).

MINIWASHITU

Gilmore, Melvin R. *Prairie Smoke.* St. Paul, MN: Minnesota Historical Society Press, 1987.

Larson, Troy. "Legend of Miniwashitu, Missouri River Monster." Ghosts of North Dakota, December 6, 2015. www.ghostsof northdakota.com/2015/12/06/legend-of-miniwashitu-missouri-river-monster (accessed March 2, 2016).

Wikipedia. "Dakota People." https://en.wikipedia.org/wiki/Dakota_ people (accessed March 2, 2016).

ALKALI LAKE MONSTER

Cryptid Wiki. "Alkali Lake Monster." http://cryptidz.wikia.com/wiki/ Alkali_Lake_Monster (accessed April 10, 2016).

Day, The. "Man Sees Antediluvian Monster, 40 Feet Long, in Nebraska", July 25, 1923. https://news.google.com/newspapers? nid=1915&dat=19230725&id=1_tGAAAAIBAJ&sjid=4fgMAA AAIBAJ&pg=2648,2307129&hl=en (accessed April 6, 2016).

Evening Independent, The. "Anglers' Club to Wage War on Nebraska's Lake Monster," July 24, 1923. https://news.google.com/ newspapers?nid=950&dat=19230724&id=uKkLAAAAIBAJ&sjid= 21QDAAAAIBAJ&pg=3974,1214487&hl=en (accessed April 6, 2016).

Morphy, Rob. "Alkali Monster: (Nebraska, USA)." Crytopia: Exploring the Hidden World, January 6, 2010. www.cryptopia.us/ site/2010/01alkali-monster-nebraska-usa (accessed April 10, 2016).

THE CLAWED GREEN BEAST

Black, T. "The Green Clawed Beast." True Tales of the Unexplained, January 15, 2015. https://ttotu.com/2015/01/15/the-green-clawed-beast (accessed April 13, 2016).

Morphy, Rob. "Green Clawed Beast: (Indiana, USA)." Crytopia: Exploring the Hidden World, December 15, 2009. www.cryptopia. us/site/2009/12/green-clawed-beast-usa (accessed April 13, 2016).

PEPIE

Lewis, Chad and Noah Voss. Pepie: The Lake Monster of the Mississippi River. Eau Claire, WI: On the Road Publications, 2014.

Ode, Kim. "Lake Pepin's rumored creature may be folklore come to life." *Star Tribune*, July 21, 2014 (accessed via http://www.startribune.com/lake-pepin-s-rumored-creature-may-be-folklore-come-to-life/267579381 on February 28, 2016).

THE MONSTERS OF DEVIL'S LAKE

Lange, Kenneth I. and D. Debra Berndt. "Devil's Lake State Park: The History of Its Establishment." *Wisconsin Academy of Sciences, Arts and Letters, Vol. 68, 1980.* http://images.library.wisc.edu/WI/EFacs/transactions/WT1980/reference/wi.wt1980.kilange.pdf (accessed March 29, 2016).

Morphy, Rob. "Devil's Lake Monsters: (Wisconsin, USA)." Crytopia: Exploring the Hidden World, October 8, 2010. www.cryptopia.us/site/2010/10/devils-lake-monsters-wisconsin-usa (accessed March 29, 2016).

Unknown Explorers. "Devil's Lake Monster." http://www.unknownexplorers.com/devilslakemonster.php (accessed March 29, 2016).

Wisconsin Department of Natural Resources. "Devil's Lake State Park: 100 Years of Stories," January 7, 2015. http://dnr.wi.gov/topic/parks/name/devilslake/history.html (accessed March 29, 2016).

THE VAN METER MYSTERY

Des Moines Daily News. "Town of Van Meter Wrought Up Over a Fishy Story: Hideous Monster Alleged to Have Terrified All," October 4, 1903.

Kilen, Mike. "Van Meter Remembers 1903 Visit from Winged Monster." *The Des Moines Register,* July 1, 2015 (originally published May 3, 2013). www.desmoinesregister.com/story/news/2015/07/01/van-meter-remembers-1903-visit-from-winged-monster/29583469 (accessed February 23, 2016).

Lewis, Chad, Noah Voss and Kevin Lee Nelson. *The Van Meter Visitor: A True and Mysterious Encounter with the Unknown.* Eau Claire, WI: On the Road Publications, 2013.

New York World. "This Monster Like a Maniac's Dream: Awful Winged Form Shedding Dazzling Light Terrifies an Iowa Town," October 5, 1903.

Saint Paul Globe, The. "A Winged Monster Creature Emitting a Dazzling Light Terrifies Hawkeyes," October 11, 1903.

THE DEMON LEAPER

Dominé, David. *Haunts of Old Louisville,* Princeton, KY: McClanahan Publishing House, 2009.

Gee, Dawne. "Tales of KY's Gargoyle Like Creature Documented in Headlines." Raycom News Network. http://raycomgroup.worldnow. com/story/25507268/demon-leaper (accessed on June 14, 2016).

New York Times, The. "An Aerial Mystery," September 12, 1880 (accessed via http://query.nytimes.com/mem/archive-free/pdf?res= 9B03E7D7143FEE3ABC4A52DFBF66838B699FDE on April 1, 2016).

Offutt, Jason. "Exploring American Monsters: Kentucky." Mysterious Universe, August 5, 2015. http://mysteriousuniverse. org/2015/08/exploring-american-monsters-kentucky (accessed January 12, 2016).

THE THUNDERBIRD ATTACKS

Before It's News. "Remember the 1977 Lawndale, Illinois Giant Thunderbird Case?" http://beforeitsnews.com/paranormal/2013/07/ remember-the-1977-lawndale-illinois-giant-thunderbird-case-2454042.html (accessed June 18, 2016).

Skygaze. "Strange and Unexplained - Thunderbirds." www. skygaze.com/content/strange/Thunderbirds.shtml (accessed March 9, 2016).

ABOUT JESSICA FREEBURG

Jessica Freeburg has always been inquisitive and loves all of the challenges that life—and the afterlife—have to offer. Her fascination with history and with the paranormal fuels many of her creative works. As the founder of Ghost Stories Ink, Jessica has performed paranormal investigations at a variety of reportedly haunted locations.

She has written young adult fiction, middle-grade narrative nonfiction and short stories for children and adults. She has served as a news correspondent for the wildly popular paranormal radio show *Darkness Radio* and on the editorial staff of *FATE Magazine*. She is the Assistant Regional Advisor for the Society of Children's Book Writers and Illustrators in Minnesota.

In addition to writing books, Jessica enjoys working in screenwriting and documentary production. She lives in Minnesota with her husband and three children. For more about Jessica and her books, visit jessicafreeburg.com.

ABOUT NATALIE FOWLER

Natalie Fowler has been fascinated by ghost stories since she was a little girl—she could never learn enough about ghosts. Once a practicing attorney, now Natalie does freelance editorial work and writes her own stories. She is a staff editor for *FATE Magazine* and Galde Press.

Natalie is a self-proclaimed research geek and could easily spend hours in the library with dusty old books. She is a paranormal investigator for Ghost Stories Ink, a group of authors and illustrators who go on ghost hunts for creative inspiration. She is always happy to fulfill any of the team's research needs.

Together with Jessica Freeburg, Natalie co-edited the group's first anthology, *Night Visions,* a collection of short stories inspired by their paranormal investigations. For more about Natalie, visit NatalieFowler.com.

MONSTERS

(OF THE)

MIDWEST

by
Jessica Freeburg
and ## Natalie Fowler

Adventure Publications
Cambridge, Minnesota

DEDICATION:

To our husbands and our children for supporting the endeavors of their slightly wacky wives/mothers. To our GSI brothers for the many fun adventures that inspire us in our craft. And to J.C. and all who love and miss him.

Edited by Ryan Jacobson

Cover design by Jonathan Norberg

Images used under license from Shutterstock.com

10 9 8 7 6 5 4 3 2 1
Published by Adventure Publications
820 Cleveland Street South
Cambridge, Minnesota 55008
(800) 678-7006
www.adventurepublications.net
Printed in U.S.A.
ISBN: 978-1-59193-647-3; eISBN: 978-1-59193-661-9